STATISTICS IN
SOCIAL WORK

STATISTICS IN SOCIAL WORK

AN INTRODUCTION TO PRACTICAL APPLICATIONS

AMY BATCHELOR

COLUMBIA UNIVERSITY PRESS | NEW YORK

Columbia University Press
Publishers Since 1893
New York   Chichester, West Sussex
cup.columbia.edu
Copyright © 2020 Columbia University Press

Library of Congress Cataloging-in-Publication Data
Names: Batchelor, Amy (Social work instructor), author.
Title: Statistics in social work : an introduction to practical
applications / Amy Batchelor.
Description: New York : Columbia University Press, [2020] |
Includes bibliographical references.
Identifiers: LCCN 2019021925 (print) | LCCN 2019981571
(e-book) | ISBN 9780231193269 (cloth) | ISBN 9780231193276
(pbk) | ISBN 9780231550222 (e-book)
Subjects: LCSH: Social service—Statistical methods. |
Social service—Practice.
Classification: LCC HV29 .B38 2019 (print) | LCC HV29 (e-book) |
DDC 519.502/4361—dc23
LC record available at https://lccn.loc.gov/2019021925
LC e-book record available at https://lccn.loc.gov/2019981571

Cover design: Elliott S. Cairns
Cover image: Leremy/Shutterstock.com

Steven Schinke (1945–2019)

This book is dedicated to the memory of Steven Schinke, PhD, D'Elbert and Selma Keenan Professor of Social Work at the Columbia University School of Social Work, who passed away on January 1, 2019.

He taught at the Columbia University School of Social Work for more than thirty years and was a dedicated researcher, teacher, and mentor. He cared deeply about the students he taught and the way he taught them. The joy he found in bringing subjects like statistics to students was infectious.

Years ago, he saw something in me, brought me to teaching, and eventually to writing this book. He did not get to see this book in print, but I wrote it with his voice in my head.

CONTENTS

Acknowledgments xi

1 INTRODUCTION 1
What Does This Book Cover? 3

2 CREATING USEFUL DATA 7
Learning Objectives 8
How Do I Use Percentages to Describe a Population? 8
What Is a Variable? 14
Levels of Measurements and How to Use Them 18
Applications in Practice 24
Key Takeaways 26
Check Your Understanding 26

3 UNDERSTANDING PEOPLE AND POPULATIONS 27
Learning Objectives 28
What Are Measures of Central Tendency? 28
What Are Outliers? 34

What Does Skew Tell Me?   43
When Would I Use Each Measure
of Central Tendency?   44
Key Takeaways   46
Check Your Understanding   47

4 **VARIANCE: THE DISTANCE BETWEEN US**   **49**
Learning Objectives   50
How Do I Measure Variability?   50
What Is the Range?   51
What Is the Interquartile Range?   52
What Is Variance?   54
What Is the Standard Deviation?   57
How Can Distributions Help Me Understand
Standard Deviation?   60
Key Takeaways   65
Check Your Understanding   65

5 **THE STATISTICS OF RELATIONSHIPS**   **67**
Learning Objectives   67
What Are Independent and Dependent Variables?   69
How Do I Measure Correlation?   70
How Do I Know How Strong a Relationship Is?   70
How Can I Understand Relationships Visually?   73
How Do I Read a Correlation Table?   78
How Can I Predict Variance?   82
How Do Statistical Models Use Relationships?   87
Key Takeaways   90
Check Your Understanding   91

6 SAMPLING: THE WHO AND THE HOW   93
Learning Objectives   94
What Is a Sample and Why Would I Need One?   94
How to Create a Sample   96
Nonprobability Sampling   96
Random Sampling   101
Random Assignment and Causality   103
What Is Sampling Error?   105
Why Is a Sample's Size Important?   106
What Is the Standard Error of the Mean
and How Do I Use It?   107
Key Takeaways   111
Check Your Understanding   111

7 WHAT WORKS?: HYPOTHESIS TESTING
AND INFERENTIAL STATISTICS   113
Learning Objectives   114
What Is a Hypothesis?   114
Considering the Means   118
How Do I Test a Hypothesis?   119
What Is a t-Test?   120
How Do I Interpret a Test Statistic?   121
What Is Statistical Significance?   123
How Do I Know If a Significant Result Is Meaningful?   126
What Do Errors Tell Me About My Results?   129
What Is the Effect Size?   132
How Do I Calculate the Effect Size?   132
Key Takeaways   138
Check Your Understanding   138

8 WHEN TWO IS NOT ENOUGH: TESTING WITH MULTIPLE GROUPS 141

Learning Objectives 141

What Is an ANOVA Test Used For? 142

How Do I Interpret a Test Statistic? 144

How Do I Use a Chi-Square Test? 149

How Do I Choose Which Test to Use? 152

Social Justice and Inferential Statistics 153

Key Takeaways 157

Check Your Understanding 157

9 AN INTRODUCTION TO ADVANCED CONCEPTS 159

Learning Objectives 159

Regression 160

More on Hypotheses: One- and Two-Tailed Tests 163

P-Hacking: The Pressure for Statistical Significance 165

Statistical Modeling 167

Bayesian Statistics: Why You'll Hear It and What You Should Know 168

Conclusion 170

Key Takeaways 171

Check Your Understanding 171

Appendix I: Glossary 173

Appendix II: Answer Key for Review Questions 181

Appendix III: Equations Cheat Sheet 187

References 189

ACKNOWLEDGMENTS

Writing this book was a labor of love for the students I teach at Columbia University School of Social Work. I could not have done it without the inspiration that they provide semester after semester.

To my editor Stephen Wesley and the editorial and marketing teams at Columbia University Press, thank you for turning my manuscript into a book. I'm sure working with a new author is never easy, and I appreciate your guidance and patience. I also want to thank Kara Maurer for her insights and feedback and Mark Perkins for being willing to triple-check my work.

Lastly, Nate, thank you for believing in me when I decided I was going to write this book, for always being happy to let me bounce ideas off you, and for talking me down when I wanted to scrap the whole thing. I would not have gotten here without you.

STATISTICS IN
SOCIAL WORK

1

INTRODUCTION

This text is written for students studying social work, with the goal of introducing important statistical concepts and tying them to the work that social workers do.

You will use statistics to help make decisions when there is uncertainty. Using observable data, statistics can help summarize and interpret what you see. When what you see is only a part of a larger whole—a sample from a population—statistics will allow you to generalize your results to the larger population.

Within the subject of statistics, understanding variables—how to track them, how they may be limited, and how their limitations affect analyses using those variables—will illuminate your own work. Understanding variables will allow you to share information about your work through a common language of statistics.

The proper use of statistics can ensure you are using evidence-based practices. Evidence-based practice has been described by the National Association of Social Workers (NASW) as "creating an answerable question based on a client or organizational need, locating the best available evidence to answer the question, evaluating the quality of the evidence as well as its applicability, applying the evidence, and evaluating the effectiveness and efficiency of the solution." To understand the evidence available and evaluate its quality, you must understand statistics. Statistics can help you vet which policies are likely to work. By collecting and using data about the populations you serve, you can use statistics to draw accurate conclusions about the efficacy of interventions or treatments. This text will give you the tools you need to understand and carry out this type of analysis.

Understanding statistics is necessary if you are to be a vigilant consumer of information, both for yourself and for your clients. Data analysis is used in everything from deciding whether someone can receive a loan to what sentence someone may receive when convicted of a crime. Therefore, social workers, especially those who work with marginalized populations, must understand how data and statistics are being used in order to be better advocates for their clients.

Even if you understand the importance of learning statistics, the language of mathematics may seem foreign and intimidating. This text will provide you with the basic statistical tools to be successful. Concepts will be described using straightforward explanations and examples that are relevant to social work. These concepts will also provide a foundation for further study in research methods and data analysis. This text is not exhaustive. It does not cover many statistical concepts found in traditional statistics courses. Instead, it focuses on applying concepts that are most useful in the context of social work.

Throughout the text, you will find examples of situations and data that are particularly relevant to social work professionals. These examples are based on direct practice working with different populations, designing or administrating social programs, and working on policy at the local, state, or federal level.

WHAT DOES THIS BOOK COVER?

The book begins with descriptive statistics. Descriptive statistics can helpfully summarize data to highlight trends that are not clear when looking at individual data points or a data table. Using descriptive statistics, you can go from a list of clients with individual scores on a measure for depression to an average score across all the clients in your caseload. You can break down a list of clients by percentages. Knowing that 80 percent of your clients are female may be more useful than just looking at a list of all your clients' names. Descriptive statistics include percentages, levels of measurement, frequencies, distributions, measures of central tendency, and variance. These tools allow you to describe a sample or a population with just a few key figures and to summarize data without pages of notes describing each individual's experience.

The next topic is correlation. Understanding correlation will help you understand the relationship between variables. "Variables" may seem like a term that does not apply to your work, but it does. Simply think of variables as inputs and outputs. For example, you might hope that by increasing the number of counseling sessions a client attends (the input, which we will call variable X) you will have an effect on your client's reported happiness (the output, which we will call variable Y). Understanding how variables X and Y are related is at the heart of your practice—and at the heart of correlational statistics.

After correlation, we cover sampling. Sampling lays the foundation for the success of any statistical test. If the sample is not representative of the population you wish to study, then the statistical tests will not help you understand the population. Deciding what type of sample is appropriate and the strengths and drawbacks of each choice will allow you to think critically about the samples used in any research you want to use to inform your work.

The last chapters of the book introduce hypothesis testing and a more complex branch of statistics called inferential statistics. Our coverage of inferential statistics includes t-tests, ANOVA, and chi-square tests. Inferential statistics are key to answering questions and doing research. Through inferential statistics you can take information you learn about a group or sample and determine what, if anything, you can say about a whole population. These chapters introduce the concept of p-values, which represent the likelihood that the values you observe in your sample have occurred by chance. This concept is essential to understanding and interpreting academic literature.

This book also introduces concepts that will help you collect and analyze data so you can track and measure your clients' progress and whether or not interventions or treatments are effective. As a clinical practitioner or program administrator, you will want to know whether what you are doing is working. You may also be asked at some point to track data for grant applications or funding solicitations or to report on progress to an agency or sponsor that is responsible for ensuring the work you do is helping the clients you serve.

The final chapter of this book introduces a few more advanced concepts that you may come across and are at the forefront of questions about the use of statistics and research in social programs and policy. These more advanced concepts include regression analysis, p-hacking, and one- and two-tailed inferential tests.

Each topic covered in this book is a tool for you to develop an evidence-based practice. Understanding statistics and research is not sufficient for evidence-based practice, but it is necessary.

Evidence-based practice involves the convergence of three distinct types of information: a practitioner's individual expertise, a client's values and expectation, and best evidence. The statistical tools you will learn in this book will make you better able to understand and evaluate what should be considered "best evidence" (Shlonsky and Gibbs 2004).

CREATING USEFUL DATA

Data are the building blocks of statistics. Without data, you cannot use statistical analysis to learn about your clients or demonstrate the effectiveness of an intervention. Data come in different forms, and the forms can limit their possible uses. Understanding what type of data you have and its limitations will help you understand the populations the data describe. Once you understand the data you can collect, you can better learn about your clients or the efficacy of a policy or program.

Data-tracking systems and new technologies are transforming social work. Data are easier to collect than ever before. Social work and human services professionals are now relying on data-driven decision-making to inform work at the program, organization, and system levels. At the program level, data might be used to track the number of family assessments completed by a team or to evaluate intentional communication techniques in a marriage counseling class. At the organization level, integrating data into, for example, a juvenile justice and reentry program's tracking system could help reduce recidivism rates by evaluating which activities have the largest effect on subsequent arrest rates. At the system level, a statewide mental health network could develop data-tracking procedure across provider networks to evaluate a new preventative counseling service. Doing so would allow practitioners and policy makers to understand the effects of the preventative counseling service on client outcomes and state dollars spent on more intensive interventions.

If you are a social worker who is working at any of these levels, you must be a good steward of the data you collect and understand how to wield those data effectively. This chapter introduces the foundational concepts for your future work with data.

LEARNING OBJECTIVES

By the end of this chapter, you should understand the following concepts:

- How percentages are calculated and used
- The relationship between proportions and percentages
- Levels of measurement and how to use them
- Which level of measurement is most useful to statistical analysis

HOW DO I USE PERCENTAGES TO DESCRIBE A POPULATION?

Data are often used in the form of frequencies or percentages. A frequency is a count of the number of times a thing occurs.

A commonly used frequency is the number of individuals or participants in a study, denoted as either N (the number of participants in a population of people or things who share a common characteristic) or n (the number of participants in a subset, or sample, of a population). Other types of frequencies involve the number of people who share a specific characteristic.

Consider a study observing the grades of eighth-grade students in New York:

- $N = 250,000$ represents the number of eighth-grade students in the state of New York.
- $n = 50$ represents the number of eighth-grade students observed in the study.
- Among those 50 students, the following frequency of grades on a reading comprehension test was observed:
  o A: 11 students
  o B: 16 students
  o C: 13 students
  o D: 6 students
  o F: 4 students

The frequency is the number of students who fall into each grading category.

A percentage (%) is a ratio that compares a number to 100. Percentages are a useful tool for describing a sample. If your sample contains 25 participants and 15 are female, then we can say that 60 percent of the participants are female. A percentage of the larger group has the characteristic of being female. Percentages make it easier to understand the makeup of a group using a single number.

To calculate a percentage, divide the value representing a subset of a larger group by the total population of the group and then multiply by 100.

For example, for the number of students who are female in the previous example, you would use this calculation:

$$\frac{\text{The number of the smaller subset of the group}}{\text{The total population of the group}} \times 100$$

$$= 15 \div 25 \times 100$$
$$= 0.60 \times 100$$
$$= 60\%$$

A proportion is a part or share of a whole and is another way to describe characteristics of a sample or group. Using the same example, if 15 members of a group of 25 are female, then it is the same as 3 out of 5 being female.

$$\frac{15}{25} = \frac{3}{5} = 0.6 = 60\%$$

If 3 out of every 5 students are female, then the ratio of female students to male students is 3:2. Out of every 5 students, 3 are female and 2 are male.

Typically, a percentage is a more useful way to characterize a subset of a sample or group. Unlike a proportion, percentages standardize the number of people with a given characteristic as a number out of 100. Standardizing results in this way makes them more easily comparable across samples, even when the sample sizes vary.

STATISTIC

In each of these examples, we have described a statistic. A statistic is a summary number that describes a sample of a population. In the preceding examples, the statistic is the percent of the sample who are female. If you want to know the gender breakdown of a sample, gender is the statistic you select.

PARAMETER

A parameter operates in the same way as a statistic, but for an entire population rather than a sample. By definition, if you are analyzing only a subset of the population for a specific characteristic, then the measure is a statistic. If you are analyzing the full population, then the measure is a parameter.

If you wanted to describe the voting record of sitting U.S. senators on a bill that would privatize Social Security, would the percentage of members voting to privatize be considered a parameter or a statistic?

Usually, capturing data from an entire population is difficult because the population is too large. Sitting U.S. senators, however, are an exception: the entire population is made up of only 100 individuals. So, in this case, you do not have to select a subset of senators who voted. You want the breakdown of votes for every single senator. Therefore, you are looking at a parameter of an entire population.

Percentages Identifying Disparities

Percentages can provide useful information about populations. Describing a population using percentages can help us understand what a population looks like, who is included, and why a population of people matters.

Review table 2.1 for an example. The data in the table describe a sample of 1,716 people who were victims of crimes. Looking at a list of each of these individuals and the characteristics that describe them would be time-consuming. Even if you looked at such a list, creating a mental image of the whole group based on that list would be difficult. A summary table that uses percentages can provide a faster and easier way to visualize the whole group.

If you looked at a list of 1,716 names followed by each person's age, race, and gender, realizing that 49 percent of the people on the list were African American would be difficult. Summary tables like table 2.1 make these data easily accessible. Knowing that a large percentage of crime victims are African American is important for understanding the crime victim population and designing better programs and policies. Maybe you know that the U.S. population as a whole is only 13 percent African American, meaning the percentage of crime victims is disproportionately (higher than would be expected given the total population) African American. This new knowledge might change your response to this information. Using percentages can easily highlight where there are inequities or disproportionate representation of certain groups.

Table 2.1 Characteristics of Crime Victims

		Number	Percent
Total		1,716	100%
Age			
	0–17	132	8%
	18–24	258	15%
	25–34	571	33%
	35–44	322	19%
	45–54	214	12%
	55–64	134	8%
	65 and over	85	5%
Race			
	Black/African American	843	49%
	White	451	26%
	Asian	230	13%
	Pacific Islander	81	5%
	American Indian	45	3%
	Other	65	4%
Gender			
	Male	954	56%
	Female	687	40%
	Other	75	4%

The utility of percentages in highlighting disparities is not limited to data tables. For example, even if you do not know how many people serve in the U.S. Congress, if you know that in 2017 only 9 percent were African American (compared to 13 percent of the population) and 21 percent were female (compared to 51 percent of the population), then you know there are disparities in this institution (Manning 2018; U.S. Census Bureau 2018). The data could be displayed in a table or not, but the message is clear either way.

WHAT IS A VARIABLE?

There are two types of variables: independent and dependent variables.

INDEPENDENT VARIABLE

An independent variable's value is not determined by that of any other variable. The independent variable is the one we manipulate in an experiment to observe an effect on a different variable we are interested in changing. For example, if you want to know how selective serotonin reuptake inhibitors (SSRIs), a type of pharmaceutical used to treat major depressive and anxiety disorders, affect levels of depression, then the dosage or type of SSRI is the independent variable. The dependent variable is the level of depression.

DEPENDENT VARIABLE

A dependent variable's value is determined in part by the independent variable. The dependent variable responds to changes in the independent variable and is considered an outcome. Any results from an empirical test (a test using observations) examine the reaction of the dependent variable to changes in the independent variable.

CRITICAL EVALUATION OF VARIABLES

Defining variables requires precise language to differentiate groups. Variables reflect human choices about how to define a group or a characteristic, so the biases that exist in human behavior can be carried over into the way that variables are defined.

For example, consider how the common definition of the variable "gender" affects our understanding. If the only options provided are "male" and "female," is anyone left out? Is anyone potentially unsure which option most accurately represents them? Does limiting the options considered limit our understanding of a spectrum of gender identity, or even mask its existence entirely? Including only two options for the variable of gender is a choice, and that choice has consequences for the types of results that are possible.

The nearly ubiquitous use of a dichotomous (meaning only two possible values) variable for gender would be extremely frustrating if you were trying to advocate for individuals who are transgender, nonbinary, or gender nonconforming. Choosing to limit the variable hides information that could be meaningful. There are plenty of variables that are not dichotomous, so working with three or more options is a regular occurrence. Why limit this variable?

Consider again the previous example in this chapter that addressed the proportion of students of each gender. The example described 15 students of 25 as female and noted that this is the same as 3 out of 5 being female, or a 3:2 ratio of female to male students. How is the discussion about these students changed if, instead, 13 students were female, 10 were male, and 2 were nonbinary? The ratios are different, but would the larger conversation about classroom makeup and student supports change as well?

As a social worker, you will find that examining variables is a chance to consider power dynamics in society. Whenever you come across a variable, whether you are filling out some sort of questionnaire or reading about a study in a popular media outlet, consider who maintains more power if the variables are defined the way they are. Does the way the variables are defined meaningfully limit the possibilities of what is considered? What is the effect of defining the variables in this way? Statistics is often presented as an exact science, but in reality statistical analyses are full of choices. Some of the earliest choices are what variables are used and how they are defined. All the choices people make filter down into the analysis that comes after. Considering the implications of the choices made at this early stage is essential to critically evaluating research.

Consider the decennial census questionnaire that shapes much of what we know about the racial makeup of the country. The categories that are included have shifted over time. For decades, the only choices were free white male, free white female, all other free persons, and slaves. When slavery was abolished, the options changed to White, Black, Mulatto, Indian, Chinese, and Japanese. Eventually, Filipino and Hawaiian were added, and Indian was changed to American Indian. Today, people can choose White; Black, African American, or Negro; American Indian or Alaska Native; Chinese; Japanese; Korean; Asian Indian; Vietnamese, Other Asian, Native Hawaiian, Samoan, Guamanian or Chamorro, Other Pacific Islander; or some other race. A separate question asks about Hispanic origin, offering the categories of Mexican, Mexican American, or Chicano; Puerto Rican; Cuban; or another Hispanic, Latino, or Spanish origin. The shifts in how data are collected has changed our understanding of who is part of the country. Having options beyond "white" or "other" reflects changing power dynamics and demonstrates the existence of greater diversity. The choices about how to define the variable of race matter for the picture we have of our country, and the decisions that are made are not neutral.

OTHER TYPES OF VARIABLES

Both independent and dependent variables can be discrete or continuous. A discrete variable is one that can only take the form of an integer or a whole number (1, 2, 3, 4, . . .). A continuous variable has an infinite number of possible values and can be described to any decimal point beyond an integer. Similarly, both independent and dependent variables can be quantitative variables or qualitative variables. Both discrete and continuous variables are numerical and therefore quantitative. Qualitative variables use words rather than numbers (e.g., mild, moderate, severe). These variables are neither discrete nor continuous. Gender is a qualitative variable where the values are words (e.g., male, female, nonbinary). The number of students in a group would be a discrete, quantitative variable because you must have a whole number of students. There cannot be 2.5 students in a class, so that variable must be an integer.

All of the terms in this section—independent, dependent, discrete, continuous, quantitative, and qualitative—are ways to describe variables.

LEVELS OF MEASUREMENTS AND HOW TO USE THEM

When thinking about variables, you should understand the level of measurement of the data that are collected. The level of measurement determines the way you can use a variable. Data can be categorized into four common levels of measurement: nominal, ordinal, interval, and ratio.

NOMINAL

A nominal variable is categorical. It may have multiple categories, but there is no value or intrinsic order to the categories. Nominal variables include gender (male/female/nonbinary), profession (doctor/lawyer/teacher), residency status (resident/nonresident), marital status (single/married/divorced), or political affiliation (Democrat/Republican/Libertarian/Green). These characteristics may be associated with numerical values for data collection purposes (e.g., 1 = single, 2 = married, 3 = divorced), but the values do not reflect anything about the data. Just because "single" is labeled with a 1 and "married" is labeled with a 2 does not mean that being single is better or worse than being married.

ORDINAL

Ordinal variables, like nominal variables, may not be associated with numerical values, but there is a clear order or ranking to ordinal variables.

Education level is an ordinal variable. An intake form for a job placement program might ask applicants to fill in their education level: less than high school, high school, college, advanced degree. These responses do not have a numerical value but there is an order to them. A college education is more than a high school education but less than an advanced degree. This is not like the nominal examples used previously. There is no order or ranking to categories of gender or to political party affiliation. You cannot say female is more or less than male, but you can say someone with a college education has received more education than someone with a high school degree.

An ordinal scale, unlike a nominal scale, can use numerical values in a meaningful way. For example, you may ask clients to rank their experience from 1 to 10. Using this scale, you would know that an experience of 4 is worse than an experience of 8. Even though this scale uses numbers, beyond the order and direction of the values, no more information is given. You are not able to say those scoring an 8 are twice as satisfied with their experience as those who scored a 4. There is not enough detail captured in this measure to know if that comparison is an accurate one.

The Likert Scale

Likert scales are rating systems often used in questionnaires and commonly used in psychology and social work to gauge clients' attitudes or feelings. Individuals or clients choose from a range of possible responses to a question or statement.

FIGURE 2.1 Likert scale

A Likert scale with five faces that range from a very sad face to a very happy face.

Some common examples are "strongly agree," "agree," "neutral," "disagree," and "strongly disagree." You can add numbers to these measures as well, linking strongly agree to the number 1 and strongly disagree to the number 5. In this case, strongly agree = 1, agree = 2, neutral = 3, disagree = 4, and strongly disagree = 5.

Figure 2.1 is an example of another Likert scale that many psychologists and social workers use, especially when working with children. This Likert scale uses faces to gain information about a person's feelings. Another common version uses faces to gauge the amount of pain a person is feeling.

Using this Likert scale, you might ask a child, "How are you feeling today?" and ask him or her to point to one of the faces. This Likert scale is ordinal. You can say that because the child selected the middle face on Tuesday but selected the happiest face on Wednesday, she was happier on Wednesday than on Tuesday. There is a ranking to the levels of happiness. However, you would be unable to say the child was twice as happy the day she selected the fourth face compared to the day she selected the second face. Ordinal measures are limited in what they can say about the relationship between values.

Each image could correspond with a numerical value. Perhaps the saddest face is equal to 1 and the happiest is equal to 5. Introducing the numerical value allows you to find an average happiness for the child over time, but to do so you must consciously assume the difference between each level is the same.

Some practitioners will assume we can say a score of 2 is twice as sad as a score of 4 in order to use more advanced statistical analysis. Others would be hesitant to ever turn these ordinal measures into interval measures because the assumption of equal values between options is too much of a stretch. You should be skeptical about assumptions regarding the values between data points and, whenever possible, avoid assumptions of equivalence where equivalence does not necessarily exist.

INTERVAL

Interval levels of measurement are the most challenging to understand. Not only does an interval scale have the directionality present in the ordinal level of measurement, but also the distance or amount between each adjacent point on the scale is the same.

The most common interval-level measurements you encounter as a social worker are in the form of standardized tests. A common example of a standardized test with an interval-level measurement is the IQ test. An IQ test works with the results from cognitive tests to create a standardized score. This score uses 100 as the average IQ and creates a normal distribution with standardized variation among scores.

Although we can describe the difference between scores of 115 and 100 as the same as the difference between 100 and 85, we cannot say that someone who scored 120 on an IQ test is twice as intelligent as someone who scored 60. To make these kinds of comparisons, there must be an absolute zero point. A zero on an IQ test, while a possible score, does not represent the absence of intelligence. An absolute zero represents a complete absence of the characteristic being measured. For these types of comparisons, we need a ratio level of measurement.

Other standardized tests you might come across in your practice include the following:

- Personality tests
- Neurological tests
- Specialized clinical tests

RATIO

The ratio level of measurement is the most useful for data analysis. Ratio measures have all the capabilities of the nominal, ordinal, and interval scales, but also have an absolute zero. Using a ratio scale allows us to make comparisons. If you can say that one value is twice as much as another, then you are working with ratio-level data.

Social workers come across relevant ratio-level data regularly. Any time you are counting—whether the number of participants in a program, the frequency of grocery stores in a neighborhood, or the days of treatment a client has received—you are interacting with ratio-level measurements. Each measurement has an absolute zero that indicates a complete absence of the object being measured.

INTERVAL VERSUS RATIO

When determining whether a variable is interval or ratio level, the key distinguishing factor is whether the variable includes an absolute zero. If a test simply includes a zero value, this is not sufficient to assume there is an absolute zero. An absolute zero is the complete absence of the object or characteristic being measured. For interval-level measurements, the zero value is arbitrarily set at some convenient or appropriate level, but the zero value does not represent the complete absence of an object or characteristic.

The Fahrenheit temperature scale is an interval-level measurement because, while there is a zero-degree point, the zero is not an absolute zero. As you may recall from your high school chemistry class, the Kelvin scale, on the other hand, has an absolute zero point where the temperature is so cold that there is a total absence of movement at a molecular level. The coldest possible temperature is 0 Kelvin. The zero on a Fahrenheit scale is not an absolute zero, so it is interval level. The Kelvin scale is ratio level because it has an absolute zero.

APPLICATIONS IN PRACTICE

Understanding levels of measurement will allow you to collect data more effectively. Knowing that nominal data can have limited utility for statistical analysis, you may instead design methods for collecting ordinal-, interval-, or even ratio-level data to allow for further analysis.

For example, while working with clients, you may want to categorize and track their happiness over time. You could start by simply noting that the client is happy one day and sad the next. But if you create a metric (or use one of the evidence-based measures available) wherein clients rank their happiness from 1 to 5 (where 1 is very sad and 5 is very happy), then you have moved from a nominal level of measurement—asking the person to respond with "happy" or "sad"—to an ordinal level of measurement.

Considering the Limitations of Variables

Defining variables is not a neutral process. Variables reflect the values, worldview, and biases of the person defining them.

Consider the challenges of studying love. How do you statistically measure the love between two people? Can love be captured in a score out of 10? Is love how many times people hug or kiss in a day? Is love how many times someone says "I love you" in a month? Do any of these successfully capture love? Can someone who does not frequently touch their partner still love them? Who would be excluded by measuring love using physical contact or verbal affirmations? Would these ways of defining love be effective across different cultures?

Many statisticians have tried to capture love in ways that lend themselves to ratio-level measurements in order to capture and analyze these data. The Love Attitude Scales (Hendrick and Hendrick 1986) use a survey of five-point scales to determine a person's style of love. This approach blends Likert scales and ratio-level data to allow for statistical analysis. The Passionate Love Scale (Hatfield and Sprecher 1986) and the Triangular Love Scale (Sternberg 1986) take different approaches to measuring love, and many others also attempt to capture this elusive feeling.

Each of these scales attempts to fit love into an easily measurable set of questions with answers that provide ratio-level data. But defining variables that can capture this phenomenon is difficult. Concepts like happiness, integrity, fairness, and justice are also difficult to turn into ratio-level data, and yet, like love, these are variables are highly relevant to social work.

Not all meaningful exploration of a subject will easily lend itself to ratio-level measurement or statistical analysis. Qualitative studies to explore complex phenomena and feelings are also necessary and useful. Qualitative observations give us insights into underlying reasons, opinions, and motivations individuals may have that cannot be captured with numbers but can be described with words.

KEY TAKEAWAYS

- Percentages are useful for summarizing information about the characteristics of a group of people or a set of items.
- Defining variables involves human choices and human biases. Examine variables to find out how they contribute to existing power structures, ignore certain groups, or shape perceptions.
- Ratio-level data are the most useful for conducting statistical analysis.

CHECK YOUR UNDERSTANDING

1. What is the relationship between a percentage and a proportion?
2. A school has 450 students enrolled, and 198 of those students receive a free or reduced lunch each day. Calculate the percent of children who receive a free or reduced lunch.
3. What levels of measurement are being used in the following examples?
    a. Gender (male/female/nonbinary)
    b. Age (in years)
    c. Level of difficulty (easy, difficult, impossible)
    d. Depression rates in a geographic region (cases per 100,000 people)
    e. Test scores (SAT score of 1250 or 1600)
4. What types of data are the most useful for conducting statistical tests?

3

UNDERSTANDING PEOPLE
AND POPULATIONS

Understanding your work with clients—whether they are students, older adults in a residential facility, individuals with a substance abuse disorder, or any other population—will involve data. The data you are most likely to use consist of information collected about individuals, such as their age, blood pressure, score on a psychological test, or the number of counseling sessions they have completed. Putting information about individuals together forms a sample. You can better understand the group beyond the individuals in it by generating some summary measures of their characteristics. When you have sample data and would like to summarize it without providing each data point, you use descriptive statistics.

In this chapter, we discuss measures of central tendency, which describe the midpoint of a dataset, and instances in which there are extreme values called outliers. Understanding descriptive statistics is the first building block for statistical analysis. Nearly every quantitative analysis of data you will encounter uses descriptive statistics.

LEARNING OBJECTIVES

By the end of this chapter, you should understand the following concepts:

- How to measure central tendency
- How measures of central tendency are affected by extreme scores
- Whether to use the median or the mean for descriptions of a distribution

WHAT ARE MEASURES OF CENTRAL TENDENCY?

Measures of central tendency identify the central number in a dataset. There are three common measures of central tendency: mean, median, and mode. You are likely already familiar with these terms. In colloquial language, "average" generally refers to the mean; in statistics, "average" can refer to any measure of central tendency, including the mean, median, or mode.

MEAN

The mean is the sum of given values divided by the number of values or scores.

$$M = \frac{\Sigma x_i}{N}$$

Where

M = the mean

x_i = individual scores or values

N = the number of scores or values for the total population[1]

The following is a hypothetical dataset for the number of months children spent in foster care before finding a permanent placement, being reunited with their family, or aging out of the foster care system:

$$5, 3, 1, 2, 0.5, 4, 2, 7, 6.5$$

To find the mean of this dataset, you would use the following calculation:

$$M = \frac{5+3+1+2+0.5+4+2+7+6.5}{9} = \frac{31}{9} = 3.44$$

You add all the scores in the dataset together (31) and then divide by the number of scores (9).

MEDIAN

The median is the middle value or midpoint of a set of values or scores. To calculate this value, you order the numbers and then find the midpoint. If there is an odd number of scores,

---

1. This may also be seen as n, which refers to the number of scores or values for a sample rather than an entire population.

this is the middle value. If there is an even number of scores, find the two middle values, add them together, and divide by two as though you were calculating the mean of those two numbers. The median can be used for ordinal- as well as interval- and ratio-level data.

We will now find the median using the same data on the number of months children spent in foster care:

5, 3, 1, 2, 0.5, 4, 2, 7, 6.5

To calculate the median value, you first order the values:

0.5, 1, 2, 2, 3, 4, 5, 6.5, 7

The middle value in this set is 3. The values 0.5, 1, 2, and 2 come before, and the values 4, 5, 6.5, and 7 come after.

~~0.5, 1, 2, 2~~, 3, ~~4, 5, 6.5, 7~~

If there were an additional child on the social worker's caseload, calculating the median would require an additional step.

If there were an additional child who had been in foster care for 6 months, then the order of values would be:

0.5, 1, 2, 2, 3, 4, 5, 6, 6.5, 7

Now there are two middle values: 3 and 4. To determine the median, add these values together and divide by two.

~~0.5, 1, 2, 2~~, 3, 4, ~~5, 6, 6.5, 7~~

$$\text{Median} = \frac{3+4}{2} = 3.5$$

MODE

The mode is the most frequently occurring value or score.

We will now find the mode using the same data:

5, 3, 1, 2, 0.5, 4, 2, 7, 6.5

The mode is the number that occurs most frequently. In this dataset, 2 is the only number that occurs multiple times. The mode here is 2.

You are most likely to use the mode when the data available are nominal or categorical. When you do not have numerical values, you cannot have a "center" in your distribution, but you may still want to summarize the data. In that case, you can use the mode.

For example, if you wanted to describe a group of people by the state where most of them live, the name of a state (New York, California, Texas) is not a numerical value. You cannot calculate a mean or a median, but you can find the state that appears most frequently. You would determine the frequency with which each state name occurs, and the one with the highest frequency would be the modal value.

If no values occur more than once, then there is no mode. If two values appear the most, then you have two modes in your dataset, or a bimodal dataset. Unlike with the median, you do not find the midpoint of two modes.

Using Descriptive Statistics as a Manager

At some point in your career, you may manage other people. You may help bring in new employees or manage a large team of people spread across different locations. When managing employees, beyond knowing about each person individually—their learning style, strengths, and weaknesses—it can be helpful to take a step back and use data to see trends across employees so you can target assistance, provide feedback, and manage more effectively.

For example, imagine you manage a team of nine case managers in a hospital. The case managers visit clients in their homes after they have been discharged from the hospital to make sure they follow their doctor's directions, attend appointments, have their prescriptions, and are connected to the services they need. You want to know the average amount of time each person spends on home visits. You have each case manager record the amount of time spent on home visits with clients each week. Table 3.1 is an example of what this might look like.

Some case managers have more clients than others. April may be new and not ready for a full caseload yet, or maybe for some reason a client no longer needed to be seen, so she does not have as many clients. This is context you add based on your knowledge of the individuals. If your goal is to have each client visited for two hours each week, you can see the average for all the hours entered by case managers is 2.18 hours, and so you know you are close to your goal.

Table 3.1 Supervisory Tracker: Hours Spent with Clients

	Client 1	Client 2	Client 3	Client 4	Client 5	Client 6	Average
April	3	4	3	2	–	–	3.00
Mario	3	1	1	4.5	2	–	2.30
Rachel	2	2	2	3	1.5	2	2.08
Whitney	1.5	0	2	2	1.5	2	1.50
Vanessa	2	2	2	2	2	2	2.00
Jared	3	4	1	2	1	2	2.17
Maria	1	3	2	1	4	–	2.20
Claire	2	3	2	2	2	1	2.00
Karina	6	3	2	3	2	0	2.67
Overall average for all client visits							2.18

You can also look at the average visit duration for each case manager. Doing so, you might see that April and Karina have higher averages than the other case managers. You know April is just getting started, so her appointments with clients are often longer, and you are not concerned. But Karina has been working for you for several years and usually has a lower average. Looking back at the time she spent with each of her clients, you can see that she spent six hours with her first client but she did not visit her sixth client. You could reach out to Karina to find out more about what caused this increase in need for her first client, in case there is a serious issue, and check in with the client who did not receive a visit.

Using descriptive statistics, you gain insights into all of the people you manage, and you can use comparisons that highlight potential problems with a quick glance at a table. The power of descriptive statistics is how much information can be shared with a few numbers. This snapshot can tell you a lot about the work you are doing and help you to do your work better.

WHAT ARE OUTLIERS?

An outlier is a value that is abnormal or distant from other observations. Outliers can dramatically alter the mean and variation of a distribution, but all outliers indicate an extreme experience. An outlier could be a valid score for someone who is an extreme case of the variable being considered. Alternatively, it could indicate that someone made a mistake and the value was recorded incorrectly. The presence of an outlier is first and foremost a cue to examine the data more carefully for accuracy and then an indication of extreme experiences.

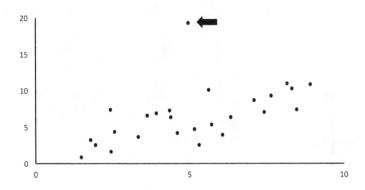

FIGURE 3.1 Scatterplot with outlier identified

A scatterplot with points clustered across the bottom of the graph and one outlier identified much higher than the other points.

In figure 3.1, one value is markedly different from the others. This is an outlier.

Consider the effect an outlier can have using the dataset we used earlier for the number of months children were in foster care (5, 3, 1, 2, 0.5, 4, 2, 7, 6.5):

$$\text{Mean} = 3.44$$
$$\text{Median} = 3$$
$$\text{Mode} = 2$$

Then consider the effect of adding an outlier.

5, 3, 1, 2, 0.5, 4, 2, 7, 6.5, 19

Looking at a graph of the data in figure 3.2, you can see that 19 is abnormal or an outlier. Maybe this value is part of the dataset as an error—someone entering the data meant to

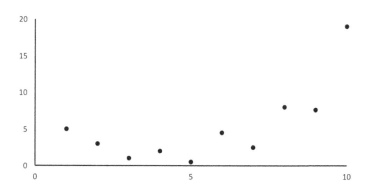

FIGURE 3.2 Scatterplot of data

Scatterplot of data including an outlier.

enter 9 but ended up entering 19 instead—or maybe this is truly an extraordinary case.

Calculate the mean:

$$M = \frac{5+3+1+2+0.5+4+2+7+6.5+19}{10} = \frac{50}{10} = 5$$

Calculate the median:

First order the values: 0.5, 1, 2, 2, 3, 4, 5, 6.5, 7, 19

Then find the middle value. Because there are 10 values, the middle values are 3 and 4.

$$\cancel{0.5, 1, 2, 2,} 3, 4, \cancel{5, 6.5, 7, 19}$$

$$\text{Median} = \frac{3+4}{2} = 3.5$$

Then find the mode:

$$0.5, 1, 2, 2, 3, 4, 5, 6.5, 7, 19$$

Table 3.2 Identifying Outliers

	Without the Outlier	With the Outlier
Mean	3.44	5
Median	3	3.5
Mode	2	2

The only value that occurs more than once is still 2.

$$Mode = 2$$

The mean is higher because of the outlier; the median is higher as well, though not by as much (see table 3.2). The effect of an outlier is largest for the mean.

In this example, the mean is greater than the median. The value of the mean moves toward the outlier. When an outlier is less than the rest of the other data points, the mean is less than the median. When an outlier is greater than the rest of the other data points, the mean is greater than the median.

There is a formula for mathematically identifying an outlier, but for your work you can usually examine the data and ensure what you are seeing makes sense. If you are interested in understanding how to calculate whether a value is an outlier, see the Equations Cheat Sheet in appendix III.

CHARACTERISTICS OF MEANS, MEDIANS, AND MODES

Once you have collected data, you can begin to analyze it. One of the first ways to examine your data is to create a

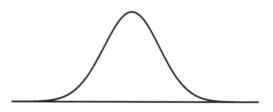

FIGURE 3.3 A normal curve

distribution. A distribution is the shape frequencies take when displayed graphically. Visualizing data using distributions highlights aspects of the data that you might otherwise overlook and makes understanding the mean, median, and mode easier. The three standard shapes of distributions described in this text are normal, positively skewed, and negatively skewed. Figure 3.3 is a normal distribution.

NORMAL DISTRIBUTION

The normal distribution, sometimes called a "bell curve" for its shape, is symmetrical around a midpoint. The majority of scores fall within an average or middle range while there are fewer values as they become more extreme. This type of distribution occurs frequently in nature, particularly given large sample sizes. Something like human height, in a large sample, would generally take this shape, with few people being very tall or very short and most people falling somewhere around the middle.

The symmetrical or "normal" distribution has the highest concentration of individuals who fall at the center of the distribution. When this is true, the mean, median, and mode are the

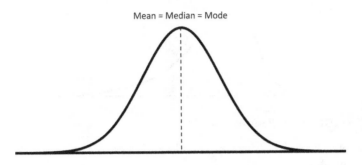

FIGURE 3.4 Measures of central tendency for a normal curve

A normal curve showing that the mean, median, and mode are all found at the highest point of the curve. For normal curves, the mean, median, and mode are all equal.

same value. Figure 3.4 is a normal distribution. When you see a data table that provides a mean and a median value, you can determine if the distribution of the data is normal by comparing the value of the mean and median to see if they are similar.

Mean = Median = Mode

POSITIVE SKEW

Figure 3.5 is a positively skewed distribution. A positively skewed distribution contains values that are higher than would occur in a normal distribution. These values pull the rightward bound of the distribution away from the normal shape.

Income is a classic example of a positively skewed variable. A few people have much larger incomes than the majority of the population, so the distribution must stretch out from the normal shape to incorporate these data points. If you were

FIGURE 3.5 Positive skew

A positively skewed distribution has a long tail on the right-hand side of the distribution.

considering an income distribution, these extremes would be people like Bill Gates and Jeff Bezos, the two richest Americans in 2017. Their incomes are in the billions of dollars each, far from the average (median) American income of about $55,000 in the same year.

For positively skewed distributions, the mean, median, and mode are not equal. The mean is more affected by extreme scores and is drawn in the same direction the data are skewed (figure 3.6). Outliers occur along the higher end

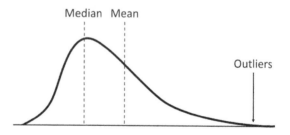

FIGURE 3.6 Measures of central tendency for a positively skewed distribution

A distribution showing where the mean and median fall on a positively skewed distribution. The median is furthest to the left, where the curve is tallest; the mean is closer to the tail, where the outliers are found.

FIGURE 3.7 Negative skew

A negatively skewed distribution has a long tail on the left-hand side of the distribution.

of the distribution. The mode will often be less than both the mean and median.

Mean > Median

NEGATIVE SKEW

Figure 3.7 is a negatively skewed distribution. A negatively skewed distribution contains much lower values than would occur in a normal distribution. These values pull the leftward bound of the distribution away from the normal shape. This type of distribution would occur for a distribution of exam scores if two students who missed many days of school in a given year failed their exams while all the students with regular attendance scored in a normal distribution. The low scores pull the distribution out of the normal shape, creating a negative skew.

When there is a negatively skewed distribution, the mean is less than the median, and outliers occur at the lower end of the distribution (figure 3.8). The mode is often greater than both the median and the mean.

Mean < Median

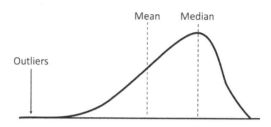

FIGURE 3.8 Measures of central tendency for a negatively skewed distribution

A distribution showing where the mean and median fall on a negatively skewed distribution. The median is furthest to the right, where the curve is tallest; the mean is closer to the tail, where the outliers are found.

You can also easily determine if a distribution is skewed by looking at a data table. Consider table 3.3. Using the data for mean and median in this table, you can determine for each variable whether the distribution is skewed.

Consider variable 1 in table 3.3, with a mean of 14.3 and a median of 6.7. There is a difference between the mean and the median, so you know the distribution is skewed. The mean is larger than the median, so the distribution is positively skewed.

For variable 3, the difference between the mean and the median is much smaller. The smaller the difference, the more difficultly you will have determining whether the values are

Table 3.3 Measures of Central Tendency

	Mean	Median
Variable 1	14.3	6.7
Variable 2	4.8	2.4
Variable 3	3.8	4.2

skewed or not. You can find the equation for determining what amount of difference is considered skewed in the Equations Cheat Sheet in appendix III.

For our purposes, we will continue to go by the much more clear-cut rules we established previously:

> If Mean = Median, then the distribution is symmetrical or normal.
>
> If Mean < Median, then the distribution is negatively skewed.
>
> If Mean > Median, then the distribution is positively skewed.

For variable 3, the mean is less than the median. Therefore, the distribution is negatively skewed, though only slightly. Even though, together, they take on the shape of a distribution, you should not lose sight of the people these distributions represent. The data points that create skew are people with extreme experiences. They may be experiencing extreme wealth, as in our previous income example, but more likely for social workers, those extremes represent people for whom a treatment did not work, who failed their exams, or who are in some way functioning or experiencing something more extreme than the people in the rest of the distribution. They are far from having the average experience. Remember that each data point you encounter, including outliers, represents a person.

WHAT DOES SKEW TELL ME?

Returning to the example of the number of months children spent in foster care, let's compare the mean, median, and mode.

5, 3, 1, 2, 0.5, 4, 2, 7, 6.5
Mean = 3.44
Median = 3
Mode = 2

In this case, 3.44 > 3 > 2, or Mean > Median > Mode. The larger values are skewing the distribution, although only a little, so the mean gives the impression that the average duration of time children spend in foster care is higher than if the distribution were normally distributed.

WHEN WOULD I USE EACH MEASURE OF CENTRAL TENDENCY?

- The mean is most useful because it allows you to do more powerful statistical tests that we will cover later in the book, but you should not use the mean if the dataset includes outliers.
- If the data are ordinal or include extreme values or outliers, use the median.
- If the only type of data available is nominal or categorical, then use the mode.

A Critical Look at Measures of Central Tendency

When you see a measure of central tendency reported, it is only as good as the data that went into it. You must think critically

---

about whether or not the measure is effective or useful for your purposes. Even trusted measures, such as the U.S. Census Bureau's measure of median income, can mask important characteristics that you should be aware of.

The definition of income used by the U.S. Census Bureau (2017) is "income received on a regular basis (exclusive of certain money receipts such as capital gains) before payments for personal income taxes, Social Security, union dues, Medicare deductions, etc."

The U.S. Census Bureau warns that this definition does not reflect noncash benefits (SNAP benefits or health insurance benefits) but includes money that individuals no longer possess because they pay it in taxes. This means someone who is wealthy and pays a lot of money in taxes but does not get many government-sponsored program benefits might have a lower net income than is represented by the Census Bureau's median. Someone with a low income from wages or salary but who receives generous government benefits might not be as impoverished as the median would lead you to believe.

You must also consider data collection methods for reported measures of central tendency. Polls or surveys are common tools for data collection, but the data are only as good as the information people are willing or able to share. Are there any reasons someone might not report information accurately on a survey? If you ask people about their annual income but they do not earn much money, might they be embarrassed and inflate their earnings? Even if people intend to be truthful, they may not remember the exact figure and give an approximation.

An example of this type of biased reporting happened in New York, where researchers found that 60 percent of people getting Temporary Assistance for Needy Families (TANF, or welfare) did not report these benefits in surveys. Program participants may feel stigma associated with receiving government services and choose not to share this information with a stranger.

The values used to calculate the mean and median affect your results. You cannot look to the reported number and simply assume it captures reality. Choices have to be made about what is and is not included. Those choices matter, and you should understand them to use the results properly.

KEY TAKEAWAYS

- Measures of central tendency are one type of descriptive statistic that can summarize larger sets of data. They help you see and understand the shape of a distribution.
- Calculating the mean requires numerical values. It cannot be used with nominal or ordinal level data. The mode is used with nominal level data and the median for ordinal level data.
- Calculating the mean involves every data point in a dataset, so extreme scores will make the mean less representative of the center point in a distribution.
- The mean is the most commonly used measure of central tendency, but the median is a better measure for datasets that have extreme scores.

Table 3.4 Client Scores on a Beck Depression Inventory

Client	Score on the Beck Depression Inventory
Client 1	9
Client 2	58
Client 3	32
Client 4	36
Client 5	49
Client 6	32
Client 7	14

CHECK YOUR UNDERSTANDING

1. Calculate the mean, median, and mode for the dataset in table 3.4.
2. Is the distribution of scores in question 1 skewed? If so, how?
3. Based on data from the U.S. Census American Community Survey shown in table 3.5, identify if each distribution would be normal, positively skewed, or negatively skewed.
   a. Households
   b. Families
   c. Married-couple families

Table 3.5 Household Income (in dollars)

	Median Income	Margin of Error	Mean Income	Margin of Error
Households	55,322	+/−120	77,866	+/−146
Families	67,871	+/−212	90,960	+/−213
Married-couple families	81,917	+/−160	106,293	+/−177

Source: U.S. Census Bureau, 2012–2016 American Community Survey 5-Year Estimates

4

VARIANCE

The Distance Between Us

The average of a dataset—whether the mean, the median, or the mode—is just one piece of information. Variability adds additional context to your understanding of a population or sample. Variability describes the extremes and the shape of a distribution. Is your distribution tightly grouped and peaked, or is it wide and flat? What does the shape tell you about the people you are working with?

By focusing solely on measures of central tendency, you neglect the extremes and get an incomplete picture of the challenges you might face. An incomplete picture also leaves you at a disadvantage when comparing groups. Groups with the same mean can have dramatically different variations. If you fail to consider variance, you might treat them in the same way when their needs are different.

LEARNING OBJECTIVES

By the end of this chapter, you should understand the following concepts:

- When you should use a range or an interquartile range
- What a standard deviation tells you about a sample
- What percentage of a distribution is included in each standard deviation from the mean
- What characteristics a curve has based on its standard deviation
- The difference between standard deviation and standard error of the mean

HOW DO I MEASURE VARIABILITY?

While measures of central tendency describe the midpoint of a distribution and can indicate whether or not the distribution is skewed, variance describes the spread or dispersion of the distribution and whether or not two distributions overlap. Understanding the overlap of distributions will be helpful later when we discuss inferential statistical tests.

There are multiple measures of variability. Some are simple, and others more complex. Some are better suited for normal distributions and others for datasets that include outliers. The most commonly used measures of variance are range, interquartile range, variance, and standard deviation.

WHAT IS THE RANGE?

A simple measure of the dispersion of a dataset is the range. The range identifies the most extreme scores and finds the difference between them. The range is the difference between the highest and lowest scores in a distribution or sample.

The formula to compute the range is:

$$R = H - L$$

Where

R = Range
H = Highest score (maximum)
L = Lowest score (minimum)

Understanding the range gives you a clearer picture of the population being described. Suppose you look at two groups of people and analyze their ages. If you find the range for one group is 45 years while the range for the other is only 5 years, then you know that these groups look different. You now know that the first group includes at least one older and one younger person but that people in the second group are all similar in age. With only information about the range, several scenarios are possible:

- One group could be of families and the other of schoolchildren.
- One group could be of all the teachers at a school, and the other could be a single classroom with 29 children and one teacher.

- One group could be the patients of a general practitioner who sees patients of many different ages, and the other could be the patients of a doctor who specializes in pediatrics.

The range uses the highest and lowest values in a dataset, so it will always pick up the most extreme values, even if they are outliers. The range cannot tell you anything about the values in between the extremes.

WHAT IS THE INTERQUARTILE RANGE?

An alternative measure of range is the interquartile range (IQR), which measures the range of the middle 50 percent of data. Combining either the range or the interquartile range with a measure of central tendency from the previous chapter, you can see how much the data vary from the mean or median. The interquartile range is more useful than the simple range when working with datasets that include outliers. By focusing only on the middle 50 percent of the dataset, you reduce the distortion outliers can create.

The formula to compute the interquartile range is:

$$IQR = Q_3 - Q_1$$

Where

IQR = Interquartile range
Q_3 = The median of the upper half of the distribution
Q_1 = The median of the lower half of the distribution

Use the following example to better understand the computation for IQR.

Find the IQR:

$$15, 10, 21, 24, 25, 4, 24, 7, 25, 16, 34$$

1. Order the values from lowest to highest.

$$4, 7, 10, 15, 16, 21, 24, 24, 25, 25, 34$$

2. Find the midpoint of the data. You can see it identified in figure 4.1 as 21.
3. Find the median of the lower 50 percent of scores. You can see it identified in figure 4.1 as 10.
4. Find the median for the top 50 percent of scores. You can see it identified in figure 4.1 as 25.
5. The value 21 is not used in either the upper or lower set of values.

$$IQR = Q_3 - Q_1$$
$$= 25 - 10$$
$$= 15$$

$$\left[4, 7, 10, 15, 16\right], \textcircled{21}, \left[24, 24, 25, 25, 34\right]$$

FIGURE 4.1 **Identifying the interquartile range**

A dataset with 11 values in which the middle number, or median, is circled and the median of the values on either side of the median are also identified, so that the IQR can be calculated.

If, instead, the IQR were 5 while the range was 30, you would know that 50 percent of your data were tightly grouped and that outliers at the upper or lower end of the distribution were contributing to the large range.

Interquartile range is often used with the median because both are better measures for datasets that have outliers.

In this dataset, the range for the middle 50 percent of data is 15. The middle 50 percent of the data has a range of 15, half the total range for the dataset (range = 34 − 4 = 30). An IQR of 15 tells you there is more variability, which is not driven by an outlier.

If two values must be averaged to calculate the median, then you include one of the values for each side of the distribution to calculate the IQR. If there were an additional value of 22 in our dataset, then the median would be 21.5 (the mean of 21 and 22).

4, 7, 10, 15, 16, 21, 22, 24, 24, 25, 25, 34

To calculate the IQR, you would include these two values.

[4, 7, 10, 15, 16, 21] [22, 24, 24, 25, 25, 34]

Then find the median for each set of values. Here, Q_1 would be 12.5 and Q_3 would be 24.5, and the IQR would be 12.

WHAT IS VARIANCE?

Variance is the average sum of the squared deviations, or differences from the mean. It is a specific measure of variability we build upon to get the more commonly used standard deviation.

The calculation for variance is:

$$Variance = \frac{\Sigma(x_i - M)^2}{n}$$

Where

Σ "sigma" indicates that you should take the sum of the terms that follow

x_i = each individual score

M = the mean of all scores

n = the sample size (this can also be seen as N, which refers to the population size)

Variance is not intuitive. The units are squared, so they do not align with units you are comfortable using. The standard deviation was created to remedy this by taking the square root of the variance to return the units to an intuitive form in which the result is in the same units (such as hours, dollars, or scores) as the original values you observed.

Measures of Variability in Practice

Imagine you have just started working at a community center developing new programs. You want to tailor the programs to fit the needs of the people who use the center. You have a spreadsheet generated from intake forms so you can learn about the people who use the center's services. The spreadsheet has the following columns:

Last name	First name	D.O.B.	Address	Phone number

You use date of birth (D.O.B.) to find the age of each person who visits the center. From there you find that the average age of visitors to the community center is 27. How do you proceed with this information?

You might guess that most people are around the mean age. If this is the case, you might develop programs for young parents, lectures on buying a first home, or résumé-writing workshops. These are programs people around age 27 might be interested in.

Instead, you decide to seek out more information before moving forward. First, you sort the list of ages from highest to lowest and find that the range is 68 years. If that is the case, then you know you have some visitors to the center who are young and some who are much older. Should you start a senior citizen exercise class and an afterschool program for children? Maybe, but maybe not. The range only tells you that at least one small child and one older adult visited the center.

Next, you calculate the interquartile range for the visitors' ages. The result is 58. There is a 58-year spread for 50 percent of your visitors. Even the middle half of your group is spread across multiple generations. Your programming is going to have to serve a wide range of visitors, from children to older adults.

WHAT IS THE STANDARD DEVIATION?

Standard deviation is the most commonly used measure of variability. Unlike variance, standard deviation has the advantage of being in the same units as the original data. As discussed above, the result of a calculation of variance might be in hours squared, dollars squared, or squared scores. The equation for standard deviation takes the square root of the variance. The square root is the only difference between the two equations, but the square root has an important function. Taking the square root of the variance returns the result to the same unit as the original values you observed (hours, dollars, or scores), making the result more intuitive.

Standard deviation is calculated using the following formula:

$$SD = \sqrt{\frac{\Sigma(x_i - M)^2}{N}}$$

Where

SD = standard deviation
Σ "sigma" indicates that you should take the sum of the terms that follow
x_i = each individual score
M = the mean of all scores
N = the population size (this can also be seen as n, which refers to the sample size).

You can break down the steps for calculating the standard deviation from this equation:

1. Calculate the mean.
2. Subtract the mean from each score.
3. Square the value of the difference between each score and the mean.
4. Sum the squared values.
5. Divide by the number of scores (at this point you have calculated the variance).
6. Take the square root of the resulting value.

Use the following example to better understand the computation for standard deviation.

Scores on an English language test for incoming asylum seekers:

$$20, 25, 29, 36, 65, 86, 89$$

First, calculate the mean for these data.

$$M = \frac{20 + 25 + 29 + 36 + 65 + 86 + 89}{7} = \frac{350}{7} = 50$$

Now, use that mean to calculate the standard deviation.[1]

$$SD = \sqrt{\frac{\Sigma(x_i - M)^2}{N}}$$

---

1. You may see equations for standard deviation that divide by $n - 1$ instead of n. Subtracting 1 artificially increases the standard deviation because you are dividing by a smaller number, making the result a more conservative estimate. While this may be appropriate in some situations, you will be well served using the equation given here.

$$= \sqrt{\frac{\begin{array}{c}(20-50)^2 + (25-50)^2 + (29-50)^2 + (36-50)^2 \\ + (65-50)^2 + (86-50)^2 + (89-50)^2\end{array}}{7}}$$

$$= \sqrt{\frac{(-30)^2 + (-25)^2 + (-21)^2 + (-14)^2 + (15)^2 + (36)^2 + (39)^2}{7}}$$

$$= \sqrt{\frac{900 + 625 + 441 + 196 + 225 + 1296 + 1521}{7}}$$

$$= \sqrt{\frac{5204}{7}}$$

$$= \sqrt{743.429}$$

$$= 27.27$$

Because the standard deviation is squared before taking the square root, the standard deviation will always be a positive value.

In this example, you can see that the standard deviation is about 27 points. Understanding that the spread of test scores out of 100 total points is +/− 27 points is intuitive.

Consider here why the standard deviation is more commonly used than the variance. The variance would be about 743. A result of 743 does not help you create a mental image of the shape of a distribution of test scores that can range from 0 to 100. This challenge is why the standard deviation is much more commonly used.

The calculation for standard deviation looks complicated, but understanding the concept of standard deviation and what it can tell you about a dataset is more important than memorizing the computation.

HOW CAN DISTRIBUTIONS HELP ME UNDERSTAND STANDARD DEVIATION?

Graphing a distribution makes standard deviation much easier to understand. In the graph in figure 4.2, the mean for the distribution is held constant at 5, but the standard deviation changes. Notice that all of these distributions are normal, with a symmetrical distribution around a midpoint. As the standard deviation changes, so does the shape of the distribution. Smaller values for standard deviation result in more peaked and thinner distributions with data concentrated around the mean. Larger values for the standard deviation result in flatter and wider distributions with more variation.

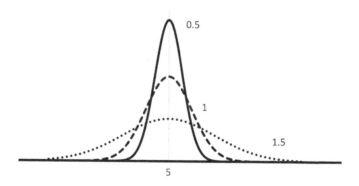

FIGURE 4.2 Varying standard deviations

Three distributions graphed on top of each other with curves that have the same median but different standard deviations. The smaller the standard deviation, the taller and thinner the curve is; the larger the standard deviation, the shorter and flatter the distribution.

Normal distributions have a constant percentage of the population between each standard deviation from the mean. The graph in figure 4.3 illustrates a mathematical fact about normal distributions and their standard deviations.

For any normally distributed dataset, about 68 percent of the sample will fall between one standard deviation above the mean and one standard deviation below the mean. About 95 percent will fall two standard deviations above and below the mean, and nearly all (99.7 percent) will fall between three standard deviations above and below the mean.

Distributions represent people, so the majority of people are within one standard deviation of the mean, and few fall more than two standard deviations from the mean in either direction.

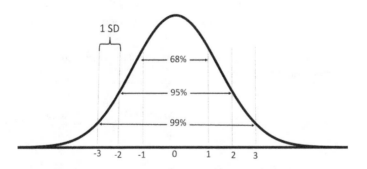

FIGURE 4.3 Area under a normal curve by standard deviations

The area under a normal curve can be divided by standard deviations. The area one standard deviation from the mean in either direction represents approximately 68 percent of the distribution. Two standard deviations include about 95 percent, and for three standard deviations it is about 99 percent.

Standard Deviation in Practice

The data in table 4.1 come from a test of a program run by the Corporation for Supportive Housing that links individuals who are frequently hospitalized and also experience homelessness to affordable supportive housing and case management services (Weitzman et al. 2017). These data are descriptive statistics for the treatment and control groups in a randomized control trial (RCT) testing the effectiveness of this type of intervention for reducing hospitalizations among this at-risk population. Those represented in the treatment column received the new care program being tested; those represented in the control column did not. Withholding the latest ideas about treatment from a portion of the sample may seem unethical, but this kind of testing is essential to knowing what works before making widespread changes to care.

Looking at this information, what can you learn about the people in the sample? What can you learn about the intervention?

Table 4.1 Treatment and Control Values for Intervention to Reduce Hospitalizations

	Treatment	Control
	Mean (SD)	Mean (SD)
Age	46.0 (10.9)	46.8 (11.5)
Medical hospitalizations	3.4 (3.6)	3.0 (3.0)
Total hospital days	14 (26.4)	16.2 (35.1)
ED visits	8.9 (11.6)	8.4 (10.9)
Psychiatric hospitalizations	0.6 (1.1)	0.5 (0.9)
Outpatient visits	40.4 (29.3)	39.7 (34.8)
Cost of care (dollars)	61,185 (38,559)	58,272 (54,789)

Focusing on outcome measures, you can apply what you know about standard deviations to imagine the shape and overlap of these distributions.

For example, for the variable "outpatient visits," the mean for the treatment group is 40.4 with a standard deviation of 29.3; for the control group, it is 39.7 with a standard deviation of 34.8. With what you know about standard deviation, you know ±1 standard deviation from the mean for the treatment group covers a range from 11.1 to 66.7, and for the control group the spread would be from 4.9 to 74.5. From these ranges, you can see that for one standard deviation, the treatment group overlaps with the control group.

A graph of the data for outpatient visits would look like the distributions in figure 4.4.

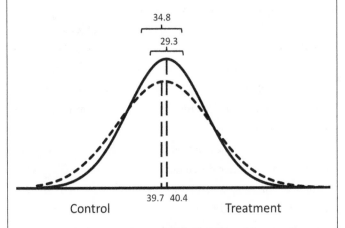

FIGURE 4.4 Outpatient visits for treatment and control groups

Distributions for the data on outpatient visits for treatment and control groups where the curves are almost completely overlapping.

You can see, even without having the tools for formal significance testing, that there is overlap between the distribution for the treatment group and the control group. The overlap is reflected in the large standard deviations.

If you randomly drew two people, one from each group, you could know how many outpatient visits they had, but you would have difficulty determining who had received the treatment and who had not based on this information alone. There is little space under each curve that is unique to either group and therefore could not possibly be part of the other.

By observing the overlap and knowing the mean and the standard deviation, you can get a sense for whether or not results are going to be significant. The more overlap there is, the less likely it is that the results will be significant. We will cover significance in much more detail in chapter 7.

You could create distributions for each outcome measure listed in the table, but because the means and standard deviations are similar, the overlap would be similar for those outcomes as well. Based on this information, what do you know about the effectiveness of providing affordable housing and case management for individuals who frequently visit the hospital? Nothing definitive, but you get the sense that the intervention did not make as much difference for the treatment group as the people conducting the experiment might have hoped. Inferential tests are required to draw conclusions from the data. You will learn more about inferential tests in the following chapters.

You can also consider how some of the curves fall below zero at the second standard deviation below the mean. Spending on hospital services cannot be negative unless the hospital pays the patient to provide services, which seems unlikely. Why, then, does the curve include negative values?

For any variable that cannot be negative (medical hospitalizations and total hospital days are other examples), if the distribution includes negative values, then the distribution must be positively skewed. Use common sense when interpreting datasets and distributions. You know patients could not have fewer than 0 days in the hospital. It is not possible. The data are skewed, and the interquartile range is a better measurement of spread in this situation.

KEY TAKEAWAYS

- Interquartile range is a better measure than range for datasets that include outliers.
- The larger the standard deviation, the larger the spread of a dataset and the flatter the distribution will be.
- About 95 percent of a sample falls within +/− two standard deviations from the mean.

CHECK YOUR UNDERSTANDING

1. Calculate the range for the following values:

    10, 92, 6, 91, 99, 12, 29, 23, 45, 51

2. Find the interquartile range for the following dataset:

23, 21, 2, 23, 23, 9, 9, 1, 12, 12, 13

3. Identify which curve has the smallest standard deviation.
   a. A normal curve
   b. A peaked curve
   c. A flat curve
4. What percent of values fall within one standard deviation of the mean?
5. Calculate the standard deviation of the following dataset:

16, 12, 19, 23, 25, 18, 1, 24, 7, 5

5

THE STATISTICS OF RELATIONSHIPS

Analyzing relationships between variables that affect people is as important as analyzing relationships between people. Correlational methods help you better understand people, communities, and policy. If you are interested in what protective factors might help develop resilience in your client, correlations help with that. If you have ever wondered whether a person's income can help predict school outcomes for their children, correlations help with that too. Or if you have ever wondered whether older adults who are lonely are more likely to experience poor health outcomes, correlations can provide useful context there too. The relationships between these variables affect the people you work with, and correlations help you analyze variables more effectively.

LEARNING OBJECTIVES

By the end of this chapter, you should understand the following concepts:

- What correlation is (and is not)
- How to determine the strength and direction of a correlation based on Pearson's r
- How to use the coefficient of determination
- How to read scattergrams and correlation tables

CORRELATION

Correlation is the statistical analysis that describes the strength and direction of a relationship between variables. As discussed in chapter 1, in your practice, you might hope that by increasing the number of counseling sessions a client attends (variable X), you will increase the reported happiness of your client (variable Y). Understanding how one variable is related to another is at the heart of your practice, regardless of the specific context you work in or the population you work with.

You must always remember that even strong correlations do not mean one variable *caused* the variation you see in the other. Correlation is not causation. If you internalize this piece of knowledge, you can be more critical of claims about research and best practices.

There may be a strong correlation between poverty levels and crime rates, but correlation does not mean that being poor causes you to commit crimes, nor that committing a crime will make you poor. Even a strong correlation should be considered carefully before you use it to justify an action. There is a relationship, but without conducting experiments, you cannot make any causal statements about that relationship.

Remembering that correlation is not causation is essential when reading or hearing about research findings, particularly research being described or summarized in nonacademic contexts. Finding a correlation between two variables and jumping to the conclusion that one must cause the other is easy to do if you are not careful. Do not to jump to these conclusions yourself.

WHAT ARE INDEPENDENT AND DEPENDENT VARIABLES?

A variable is an entity that is being measured. There are two kinds of variables: independent and dependent.

- An independent variable (x) is the input, the one that is manipulated in a scientific experiment, or one that is stable and unaffected by the other variables you are trying to measure.
- A dependent variable (y) is the output, the one that has a consequent role in relation to the independent variable; changes made to the independent variable affect the dependent variable.

For example, in a comparison of income and poverty, income is the independent variable. Poverty is the dependent variable because a person's income level determines whether that person is above or below the poverty line.

In a clinical setting, the dose of an antianxiety medication is the independent variable, and level of reported anxiety is the dependent variable. Adjusting the dose of the medication should affect the level of anxiety. The level of anxiety is dependent on adjusting the dosage of medication to find the best fit.

HOW DO I MEASURE CORRELATION?

Pearson's r, also known as the Pearson product-moment correlation coefficient, was named for British statistician Karl Pearson. Pearson's r is a common statistical tool you will come across in academic studies. As its name suggests, r is a measure of correlation. Specifically, Pearson's r creates a scale for understanding how correlated two variables are with each other.

For your social work practice, understanding and interpreting Pearson's r is more important than being able to calculate it.

HOW DO I KNOW HOW STRONG A RELATIONSHIP IS?

Pearson's r measures both the strength of a relationship and its direction.

- Pearson's r can only have a value between -1 and 1.
- The strength of a relationship is determined by the distance of r from 0, or the absolute value of r.
- The direction of a relationship is determined by whether the value is positive or negative (figure 5.1).
- If Pearson's r is equal to 1, then the relationship is a perfect (very strong) direct relationship.

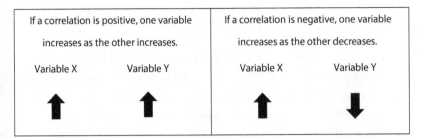

FIGURE 5.1 **Relationships and correlation**

When a correlation is positive, one variable follows the other. If one increases, the other increases. If one decreases, the other decreases. This is a direct relationship. When a correlation is negative, one variable behaves the opposite of the other. If one increases, the other decreases. If one decreases, the other decreases. This is an inverse relationship.

- If Pearson's r is equal to -1, then the relationship is a perfect (very strong) inverse relationship.
- If Pearson's r is equal to 0, then there is no relationship.

Consider the values for the strength of a relationship as though they fall on a scale like the one depicted in figure 5.2.

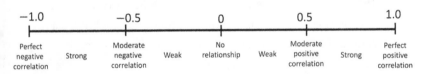

FIGURE 5.2 **Measuring magnitude of Pearson's r**

A scale for measuring the magnitude of Pearson's r where one end begins with -1.0 and a perfect negative correlation and the other end is 1 with a perfect positive correlation. In the middle is a 0 where there is no relationship at all and between the ends and the middle there are strong, moderate, and weak levels of correlation.

SPURIOUS CORRELATIONS

A relationship with either a perfect correlation (1 or −1) or no correlation at all (0) is rare. Some variables are correlated even though no causal relationship exists. These correlations are called spurious correlations. A spurious correlation is misleading because the r value indicates that a correlation exists between two variables but the correlation is produced through the operation of a third causal variable that is not examined by the analysis, or the correlation may be due to random chance.

For example, the number of marriages in Alabama is correlated with the annual deaths caused by lightning strikes in the United States at $r = 0.89$ (Vigen 2015). You just learned that $r = 0.89$ is considered a strong positive correlation. As more people get married in Alabama, it must be more likely people in the United States will be struck by lightning. Could the number of people who get married in Alabama somehow cause more lightning strikes? Or could the fear of getting struck by lightning cause more people in Alabama to propose? This relationship does not make sense. When a relationship does not make sense, you should look for other possible explanations. Here are two possible explanations in this case:

- A third variable, population, is driving the relationship. The increase in population is leading both to more marriages in Alabama *and* to more people who could potentially be struck by lightning.
- Random chance caused these two values to increase at the same time.

Another example of spurious correlation in the social work literature has to do with the relationship between family income and child development. Researchers have argued that income effects are driven by unmeasured factors that are correlated with both income and child outcomes but are not captured when simply looking at income and child development. They argue that rather than income driving the relationship, factors such as parental mental health or motivation drive earnings and also affect child development. The underlying relationship between these other factors leads to a spurious correlation between income and child development (Magnuson and Votruba-Drzal 2009).

If family income has a spurious relationship with child development, the types of interventions you would consider to improve child outcomes are different. Instead of focusing on connecting families to cash assistance programs or helping parents find jobs, you would prioritize addressing any mental health challenges that may be driving both income insecurity and poor child development.

HOW CAN I UNDERSTAND RELATIONSHIPS VISUALLY?

You can understand correlations visually using a scatterplot or scattergram—a diagram or graph that plots variables to show their relationship. Figure 5.3 shows examples of this type of graph.

In figure 5.3, the left graph shows an example of a strong positive or direct correlation ($r = 0.96$, very close to 1). The

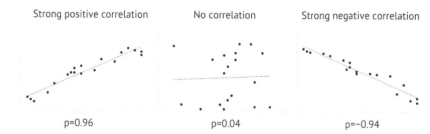

Strong positive correlation   No correlation   Strong negative correlation

p=0.96   p=0.04   p=−0.94

FIGURE 5.3 Understanding correlation using scatterplots

Three graphs showing strong positive correlation, no correlation, and strong negative correlation. The positive correlation has fairly closely clustered data around an upward-sloping line with $r = 0.96$. No correlation has data points scattered in a way that appears random, with no clear clustering of points and an r of 0.04. The negative correlation has fairly closely clustered data around a downward-sloping line with $r = -0.94$.

values of one variable increase with the values of the other variable. For example, this could show the relationship between years of education and income. As the number of years people spend in school increases, so does their eventual annual income, with individuals who have advanced degrees earning the highest incomes. One variable increases (education level measured by number of years) as the other increases (annual salary measured in dollars).

The second graph shows an example of no correlation. While r is not quite zero, this is a *very* weak correlation ($r = 0.04$). No relationship exists between the two variables plotted here. Even though a trend line is included, you see no clear pattern in the points. This could show the relationship between the amount of coffee people drink and the number of pets they own. One variable (coffee consumed measured in ounces) does not increase or decrease in the same way the other variable (pets measured as the number of cats, dogs, birds, etc.) does. We would expect no relationship to exist between these two variables.

The final graph in figure 5.3 shows an example of a strong negative or inverse correlation ($r = -0.94$, very close to -1). The values of one variable decrease as the values of the other variable increase. This could show the relationship between college GPA and alcohol use. As the amount of alcohol regularly consumed by college students increases, the value of their GPA decreases. One variable increases (alcohol consumption measured in number of drinks), but the other decreases (GPA).

Not all relationships are so clear, with either a strong or weak correlation. In figure 5.4, the relationships are much weaker than those shown in figure 5.3. In figure 5.4, despite

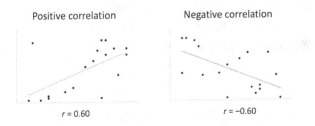

FIGURE 5.4 Scatterplots for moderate correlations

Two graphs showing moderate positive and negative correlations. The positive correlation has some data points that are closely clustered around an upward-sloping line but others that are further from those clusters; $r = 0.6$. The negative correlation has some data points that are closely clustered around a downward-sloping line but others that are further from those clusters; $r = -0.6$.

some outliers and no tightly clustered points, the r value is still 0.6 or −0.6, a moderate correlation.

When you analyze correlation data, you must understand the relationship between the strength or magnitude of a correlation and the direction of the correlation. Of the following r values, which has the stronger correlation?

$$0.34 \quad \text{or} \quad -0.45$$

The value of $r = -0.45$ is a stronger correlation than $r = 0.34$.

You first use the absolute value of r to determine the magnitude of a correlation and then take into account the direction of the relationship between the variables. The absolute values here are 0.34 and 0.45, and 0.45 is stronger than 0.34. A negative sign before the value for r does not affect the strength of the relationship, only the direction. If there is a negative sign, then you know the relationship is inverse. Without a negative sign, the relationship is direct or positive.

Correlations, Risk, and Resilience

Much of what we know about mental illness, particularly about the risk and resilience factors, is based on studies of correlations between diagnoses and genetic and environmental factors. As a social worker, you will use the results of correlational research to inform your work with clients and to shape your practice.

Consider the following statements from an article in the journal *Social Work Research*:

Risk factors are markers, *correlates*, and—in a best-case scenario—causes. For example, although other factors are related to serious mental illnesses such as schizophrenia, parental psychopathology is thought to influence the likelihood of developing the disorder. How it does that—whether through genetic or environmental influences—is not yet fully understood. But the word "risk" denotes the fact that a group of people with a similar characteristic is more likely than others in the population at large to develop a problem (in this case, schizophrenia). (Fraser, Galinsky, and Richman 1999, 131–132; emphasis added)

The article is describing correlational research. There is a relationship between mental illnesses such as schizophrenia and whether parents have also experienced a mental illness, but setting up experiments to find a causal relationship is impossible. You cannot control who a person's parents are, nor whether they have a mental illness. Instead, once an individual has been diagnosed later in life, researchers can look back at factors from the person's childhood, or at the person's lifestyle for environmental factors, but cannot limit or control factors in the person's life to set up a more rigorous experiment. Correlation does not guarantee there is a causal relationship, but when you cannot achieve causal results, correlations can create a body of useful literature for practitioners to draw from.

The article goes on to describe some risk factors that are correlated with mental health disorders:

> Some individual, familial, and extra-familial factors appear to affect many disorders concomitantly and in that sense, they are "nonspecific" risks. They elevate risk for a variety of conditions. These risk factors include child abuse; chronic family conflict; unskilled parenting; academic failure; peer rejection; poverty; racism, sexism, and other types of discrimination; and neighborhood disorganization. (Fraser et al. 1999, 132)

Imagine you are working in a high school. You know from this article that parental psychopathology is correlated with mental illness and that experiences of child abuse, academic failure, and poverty are also correlated with higher risks. This knowledge could help you prioritize students for mental health screenings and early intervention. It could lead you to include questions on your intake form about students' family history with different conditions. If you work in a school where poverty and racism are common experiences, this correlational research may motivate you to develop resilience tools and training for students to mediate some of these risk factors.

HOW DO I READ A CORRELATION TABLE?

Scholarly articles that discuss correlation often include a correlation table or correlation matrix. Table 5.1 is an example

Table 5.1 Correlations Among Variables

	1	2	3	4
1. Poverty	1	0.24	0.20	0.70
2. Population	0.24	1	0.53	0.15
3. Violent crime rate	0.20	0.53	1	0.26
4. Unemployment rate	0.70	0.15	0.26	1

of a correlation table. You may have never seen a table like this, but it can provide a lot of information.

First, notice that there are numbers beside each variable name and along the top of the table. This is a common shorthand used in correlation tables instead of including the variable names in the table twice. When there is a 1 at the top of the table, it is in place of "Poverty." This method allows the author to save space, but the numbers could be replaced with the name of the variable without changing the results in the table.

Notice that the number 1 is repeated along the diagonal; in other tables, these 1s may be replaced with dashes or blank spaces. The 1 occurs when a variable is compared to itself. For example, where "Violent crime rate" and column 3 meet in the table, there is a 1, indicating a perfect correlation between these two variables because they are the same variable. In figure 5.5 the 1s are highlighted for when a variable is compared to itself.

To find the value of the Pearson's r for each set of variables, you find the intersection where the two variables meet. In figure 5.6, you can see that if you want to find the r value for the relationship between Poverty and Violent crime rate

	1	2	3	4
1. Poverty	1	0.24	0.20	0.70
2. Population	0.24	1	0.53	0.15
3. Violent crime rate	0.20	0.53	1	0.26
4. Unemployment rate	0.70	0.15	0.26	1

FIGURE 5.5 Perfect correlations in a correlation table

A correlation table highlighting the places where a variable intersects with itself in the table and therefore has a perfect correlation. Where this happens, a 1 is shown in the table, and those 1s create a diagonal line through the center of the correlation table.

(indicated by the number 3 at the top of the table), you find the point where the row and column intersect. In this case, the intersection point is at $r = 0.20$.

You may also see data tables that looks like table 5.2.

In this table, half of the table is left blank because the values simply repeat those listed in the lower half of the table.

	1	2	3	4
1. Poverty	1	0.24	0.20	0.70
2. Population	0.24	1	0.53	0.15
3. Violent crime rate	0.20	0.53	1	0.26
4. Unemployment rate	0.70	0.15	0.26	1

FIGURE 5.6 Finding correlations in a correlation table

A correlation table indicating the intersection between the variable Poverty and the variable Violent crime rate. The row for Poverty is highlighted, as is the third column, which corresponds to Violent crime rate. The Pearson's r for this relationship is found where the two highlighted areas cross.

Table 5.2 Correlations Among Variables

	1	2	3	4
1. Poverty	–			
2. Population	0.24	–		
3. Violent crime rate	0.20	0.53	–	
4. Unemployment rate	0.70	0.15	0.26	–

All the information represented in table 5.1 is still present in table 5.2, but repeating values are only displayed once. If you look again at table 5.1, you will notice that if you find where Poverty intersects with column 3 for Violent crime rate, it is 0.20. If you follow Poverty in row 1 to column 3 for Violent crime rate in table 5.2, you will not find a value. Instead, follow row 3 for Violent crime rate to column 1 for Poverty to find the same 0.20.

	1	2	3	4
1. Poverty	1	0.24	(0.20)	0.70
2. Population	0.24	1	0.53	0.15
3. Violent crime rate	(0.20)	0.53	1	0.26
4. Unemployment rate	0.70	0.15	0.26	1

FIGURE 5.7 Mirrored data in correlation tables

In a correlation table, there are two places where the same variables intersect. When looking for the relationship between violent crime and poverty you can either go to the first row for Poverty and the third column for Violent crime rate to find the Pearson's r, or you can look at the third row and the first column. The values you find in these two locations will be the same.

HOW CAN I PREDICT VARIANCE?

You may want to use correlations to predict what will happen in the future rather than examine what has already happened. Pearson's r cannot help with this, but the coefficient of determination, referred to as r^2, can.

Variance is simply a measure of how much a set of numbers differs from their average value. The coefficient of determination determines the proportion of the variance in the dependent variable that is predictable from the independent variable. For example, the coefficient of determination might indicate that an increase in the amount of exercise people do each day can predict 20 percent of the change in their weight over a given period of time.

The calculation for r^2 is relatively simple. Once you find the value of r, you square this value. Because all r values are between -1 and 1, the squaring operation results in a smaller value for r^2 than for r. Suppose, for example, that $r = 0.65$.

$$r^2 = 0.65^2 = 0.65 \times 0.65 = 0.42$$

When $r^2 = 0.42$, then 42 percent of the variation in one variable is predicted by the variance in the other variable, or one variable is 42 percent effective at predicting the other.

Setting Priorities Using the Coefficient of Determination

Often social workers have to make choices about how to target services. Resources are limited, and they need to be used effectively. Understanding correlations and coefficients of determination can provide context for decisions about how to use scarce resources.

For example, if you work for an organization that addresses intimate-partner violence (IPV) and you want to start a prevention program, what population should you focus your resources on? You may not have the capacity to serve everyone. Is there a way to target your services to have the greatest effect?

Some studies have tried to find predictive variables for the incidence of IPV. These studies looked for relationships among variables such as education level, employment status, self-esteem, experience or viewing of domestic violence as a child, previous criminal justice system interactions, and many other factors. If you can only serve a limited number of people, what factors should you prioritize to increase the likelihood of achieving your goal of decreasing IPV in the future?

If the education level for your potential participants varies, you can look at the correlation between education level and incidences of IPV.

Suppose a study found $r = 0.60$ for incidence of IPV and partner education level.

$$r^2 = 0.60^2$$

$$r^2 = 0.60 \times 0.60$$

$$r^2 = 0.36$$

So, a partner's education level can account for 36 percent of the variation in incidence of IPV. A partner's education level may not be the best way to prioritize participation in the program, but in social science 36 percent is quite strong.

Another study found $r = 0.77$ for experiencing physical abuse in childhood and being abusive as an adult.

$$r^2 = 0.77^2$$

$$r^2 = 0.77 \times 0.77$$

$$r^2 = 0.59$$

Therefore, experiencing abuse in childhood can account for 59 percent of the variation in being abusive as an adult, a much higher percentage than education level. While 59 percent may not seem like a strong predictor, in social science this is considered a strong result.

Given this information, you might prioritize potential clients who report experiencing abuse in childhood over those who do not report experiencing abuse in order to better target your resources. You should consider the implications of using predictions like this, though. Many predictions use data about relationships that are based on behaviors of groups of people and not the individuals themselves. In this case, targeting people to receive additional services can be helpful. Using the same information in a punitive way, such as denying someone custody of her children, is unethical. While being abused as a child *in general* leads to a higher risk of perpetrating abuse as an adult, it does not predict any one individual's likelihood of perpetrating abuse.

In summary, these are some of the characteristics of r^2:

- The value of r^2 ranges from 0 to 1.
- If the value of r^2 is 0, then the dependent variable cannot be predicted using the independent variable.

- If the value of r^2 is 1, then the dependent variable can always be predicted without error using the independent variable.

- Any value for r^2 indicates what percent of variance in the dependent variable can be predicted using the independent variable.

- If r^2 is 0.5, then 50 percent of the variation in the dependent variable can be predicted using the independent variable. An r^2 of 0.6 means that 60 percent can be predicted, and so on.

Again, correlation is not causation, but understanding these relationships and where strong or weak relationships exist can help you tailor more effective interventions, or at least better understand the individuals or populations you are working with.

There are limitations to using r^2. To use r^2, the relationship must be linear. If the data are curvilinear, r^2 is no longer an appropriate tool. If you graph your data on a scatterplot and find that they resemble the curvilinear graph in figure 5.8, you cannot use r^2 to assess your data.

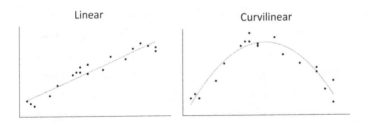

FIGURE 5.8 Linear and curvilinear distributions

On the left is a linear distribution, with data points on the scatterplot clustering along a straight upward-sloping line. On the right is a curvilinear distribution, with data values on the scatterplot beginning in the lower left-hand corner, increasing, and then decreasing, to cluster around a curve.

Out-of-the-Box Relationships

Correlations are limited by the relationships you test. When you look for relationships, you may miss factors you do not expect to find.

This limitation played out on a national scale through the 1980s and 1990s. These decades saw a considerable increase in crime rates across the United States. Crime can have many negative effects on communities, victims, perpetrators, and their friends and families. Politicians and policy makers were determined to figure out the cause of this rise and to reverse it.

Dozens of studies were published on the correlation between poverty and crime. These studies found correlations ranging from as low as 0.05 to as high as 0.75. A review of many of them found the weighted average estimate for correlation between violent crime and poverty was 0.44 (Hsieh and Pugh 1993)

Other relationships that were studied included the now popularly known "broken windows" policing strategy, in which less serious crimes were targeted as a way of reducing more serious crimes (Kelling and Sousa 2001). Two economists suggested that crime dropped later in the 1990s because of *Roe v. Wade*: legalized abortion, they argued, led to fewer unwanted babies, which meant fewer young men with risk factors for criminal activity (Donohue and Levitt 2001).

Then research from a different field linked exposure to lead to problems with mental development. A study suggested a link between children's exposure to leaded gasoline and crime twenty years later as those children grew up (Nevin 2000). This study found that lead emissions from automobiles accounted for 90 percent (r^2) of the variation in violent crime.

The relationship between environmental toxins and crime was not obvious. Yet this relationship explained more of the rise in violent crime than all of the other factors considered and had very different policy and prevention implications.

HOW DO STATISTICAL MODELS USE RELATIONSHIPS?

As computers have made analyzing large amounts of data and identifying trends easier, an increasing number of decisions are made based on relationships. Predictive models that use correlations, among other things, have become popular for everything from optimizing online advertising to determining how long a person will spend in prison. You must understand that those correlations are not causal, and choosing which relationships to prioritize has implications that could affect your clients.

Models are just opinions fixed in mathematics. By choosing which relationships to prioritize and which to ignore, people are deciding what is important to them. Nothing about statistics is completely neutral. Understanding the limits of these relationships when working with correlations can help you defend against improper use of them in much more complex mathematical models.

A model that predicts someone's risk for committing a crime based on factors such as whether or not they had interactions with police from a young age or whether the people close to them have been convicted of a crime can seem like a reasonable way to determine risk. However, because of discrimination that has affected marginalized communities, the algorithm disproportionately predicts that black men are at higher risk for offending. Policing policy across the country has meant that young black men are more likely to interact with police from an early age because a higher concentration of police presence in predominantly black areas increases the likelihood of interactions compared to majority-white neighborhoods (Skogen and Frydl 2004). The model may not specifically ask about race and then correlate it to risk, but if enough of the relationships vary based on race, the model can further disadvantage already marginalized populations.

As a social worker, understanding correlation and its limitations can prepare you to engage with models that often *look* neutral and to advocate for your clients when the models are unfair or biased.

Any time you are faced with a statistical model based on correlation, relationships, or trends, ask yourself some questions like these:

- Could any of the variables being used be substituted for race? If instead of looking at that variable, someone simply looked at race, would the results be the same?
- What about wealth or poverty?
- What about gender?
- Will the results always disadvantage an already marginalized group?

Not enough social work organizations work with statisticians to ensure that they consider social justice norms when setting up models. Your local government may be trying out a new predictive crime model, or developers in your area could design an algorithm to help identify child abuse. Bringing a social work lens to statistics is an outsized opportunity to affect the lives of people who will eventually feel the impact of those models. Being comfortable with basic statistical concepts is the first step to engaging in these important discussions.

Making Just Hiring Decisions

Regardless of the type of work you would like to do, you will almost certainly find yourself in a workplace where decisions are made about hiring. Hiring employees has lasting implications for those who are hired and for those who are not.

Social workers can advocate for social work values in the hiring process, especially if your employer is using a statistical model to predict employee suitability.

Many software programs offer the promise of simplified, less time-consuming hiring. These programs generally use trends and correlations to identify qualities such as dependability, likelihood of staying with the employer for a long time, education level, comfort level interacting with people, or any number of other variables to select a small subgroup of applicants for a closer look. As discussed in the previous chapter, variables like dependability or comfort interacting with people are difficult to turn into ratio-level data and therefore difficult to put into models. Instead, the model might use a variable that is easy to incorporate, such as credit score or number of connections on social media.

Social workers should consider how these factors might unfairly disadvantage some individuals. How would limited access to a computer hamper a person's ability to build extensive connections on social media? Would this metric disproportionately disadvantage people with lower incomes? How might historical discrimination contribute to lower credit scores for black or Latino applicants? Neither of these variables measures a skill that is directly applicable to a job. Yet they can be included in hiring models and perpetuate a cycle that disadvantages individuals who already face challenges. Bringing a social work lens to this seemingly unrelated field can lead to fairer hiring decisions, a more diverse pool of candidates, and less inequality in the system.

KEY TAKEAWAYS

- The strength of a correlation does not depend on whether it is a positive or negative number. When $r = -0.78$, it is a stronger correlation than $r = 0.55$.
- A coefficient of determination (r^2) can tell you the percent of the variation in the dependent variable that is predicted by the independent variable.
- Correlation is not causation. Knowing there is a relationship does not tell you if one variable caused the behavior of the other.
- Understanding correlations can be a foundation for evaluating statistical models through a social justice lens.

CHECK YOUR UNDERSTANDING

1. In each of the following pairs of values for r, which is the stronger relationship?
   a. 0.01 or 0.45
   b. −0.53 or 0.67
   c. 0.48 or −0.72

2. Find the percentage of variance predicted by the independent variable using the following values for r (round to the nearest percent).
   a. $r = -0.23$
   b. $r = 0.67$
   c. $r = 0.04$
   d. $r = -0.89$

Use Table 5.2 (page 81) to answer questions 3–6.

3. What is the value of r for the relationship between the unemployment rate and poverty?
4. Population size predicts what percent of violent crime?
5. Poverty is most strongly associated with which variable?
6. Which relationship has the weakest correlation?

6

SAMPLING

The Who and the How

Anytime you are interested in learning about a group, you will make observations or do tests with members of that group. The group you are interested in might be an entire population or a specific group such as teenagers, new mothers, or people who have been diagnosed with depression. Without access to every member of the group you are interested in, you will rely on samples. The strength of your sample—how closely it represents the larger group you are interested in—determines the reliability of your conclusions.

Even if you never plan to do research or cannot imagine a situation in which you would create a sample, you will rely on research and best practices that were tested with samples. Does the sample that was used look like the group of people you work with? If the sample was not representative, then you cannot assume the results will occur for the group you are working with. If you understand how to evaluate samples, you will be better able to serve your unique client population. A sample of individuals who live in urban areas would not be applicable for a primarily Native American population living on a remote reservation. If you served this population, you would not want to assume the conclusions were relevant to your work.

LEARNING OBJECTIVES

By the end of this chapter, you should understand the following concepts:

- How samples are selected
- How to identify biases in a sample
- How to understand the implications of sampling error
- How sample size affects results

WHAT IS A SAMPLE AND WHY WOULD I NEED ONE?

Many questions you want to answer start with a group you are interested in. Maybe you are interested in working with older adults, maybe you are interested in working with teenagers, or maybe you are interested in working with elementary school children. Each of these groups of interest is a population. You may be interested in just the population of older adults who have dementia, or you may be interested in an even smaller group of females with dementia living in the assisted living facility where you work. In these examples, you can see the scope of the population you are interested in can be inclusive or narrow. Your use of statistics will start with a population.

POPULATIONS AND SAMPLES

A population consists of *all* members of a group, whereas a sample is a *part* or subset of a population. If you are looking at an entire population and there is a difference between two groups within the population, then there is a real difference. The difference may be small and may not be clinically significant, but it is real. When you begin to work with samples, or portions of the population, determining if a difference is real is not so straightforward.

If you are studying the population of females with dementia living in assisted living facilities and you select 100 females from the 10 closest assisted living facilities, then you have created a sample. You are no longer testing *all* the individuals in the population; you are focusing on a smaller portion of the larger group and treating them as representative of the larger group.

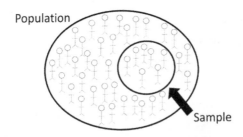

FIGURE 6.1 **A sample within a population**

A large group of people fall within a circle identified as a population. A smaller circle inside the circle for the population identifies a set of people who are selected as a sample of the population.

No matter what type of sample you select or how you choose the people to be in your sample, your sample may not accurately reflect the characteristics of the larger population. You can select a sample to minimize risk, but risk is always present.

Why would you want to use a sample if it might not be representative? Often you face time or resource constraints that make testing an entire population impossible. You may be interested in how children's academic performance is affected by placement in foster care. According to the U.S. Department of Health and Human Services (2017), there were 437,465 children in foster care in the United States in 2016. Surveying each child would be difficult or impossible, and setting up an experiment to test an intervention would be time and resource intensive. Your best alternative is to create a smaller sample to work with.

HOW TO CREATE A SAMPLE

There are two main types of sampling: nonprobability and random sampling.

NONPROBABILITY SAMPLING

A nonprobability sample is any type of sample that does not give every member of the population an equal chance of being selected. Nonprobability sampling includes convenience sampling, volunteer samples, purposive samples, and snowball sampling.

CONVENIENCE SAMPLING

Convenience sampling uses individuals who are, as the name suggests, convenient or easy to access. If you are working at a university, creating samples from the students at the university where you work is relatively easy. If you want to get the opinions of people who live in New York and you talk to everyone who walks past you on a street corner in Brooklyn, then you are creating a convenience sample.

Now consider the factors that might affect the composition of the group of people you speak to. Are you out on a weekday during the day? You might be talking to people less likely to have jobs keeping them at work and off the street during the day. Is the neighborhood more residential, or are you standing at a busy corner where there are lots of stores? How would where you are standing affect who happens to walk by? Many factors could bias the sample of people you encounter. Standing on the corner talking to people is much easier than carefully constructing a representative sample, but there are limitations to what you can say about the residents of the city based on the people you spoke with.

Is Everyone Like a Student?

You just learned about sampling and the importance of constructing a representative sample. So, you may be surprised that much of what we believe about human psychology, economics, and cognitive science is not very representative at all. From

2003 to 2007, an analysis of academic journals studying these topics revealed that 68 percent of participants came from the United States, and 96 percent were from Western industrialized countries (Henrich, Heine, and Norenzayan 2010).

In a study of psychology journals, Jeffrey Arnett (2008) found that 67 percent of American studies published used undergraduate psychology students for their sample. If psychology as a field were particularly interested in the behavior of university students, this type of sample still might not be valid. Do psychology students differ in meaningful ways from engineering students or art students? Is the distribution of gender representative? To draw conclusions about human behavior across all ages and geographies based on the behaviors of largely 18- to 25-year-old university students is not credible.

Why would these studies rely heavily on a particular group of people if they are not representative of the larger society? Likely, because it is convenient. If you are at a university doing research and teaching classes, you have easy access to students. You do not have to use many resources to find participants. This is a clear case of convenience sampling.

Who is included in a sample has a meaningful effect on how useful the results are for larger populations. You would not want to assume that counseling tested with college students would be successful with older adults. Nor that treatment tested only on American university students would necessarily be successful with students in Kenya or India. Carefully examine the makeup of samples before trusting that the results based on those samples will be useful to you and your practice.

VOLUNTEER SAMPLES

Another straightforward way of finding participants is to accept volunteers. People who are able and willing to participate in a survey or study can self-select into doing so. You get the participants you need, but using this kind of sample leads to a problem called volunteerism. If you post an advertisement in city buses and subway stations with a phone number to call to be screened for a study on family conflict and then wait for people to volunteer, are the people who call going to be a representative group? Are individuals who have strong feelings on this topic more likely to participate, or are people who are especially enticed by the pay they receive for participating more likely to take the time to call? What about people who do not take the bus or subway? Those families will not have seen the advertisement and will be left out entirely. Volunteerism is a source of bias based on the differences between people who are able and willing to volunteer and those who are not.

PURPOSIVE SAMPLING

A purposive sample is another type of nonprobability sample. Unlike convenience samples, purposive samples are selected in a deliberate but not random way to find people who can provide specific information or have specific experiences that are needed for the work.

If you want to study resilience and motivation among female CEOs for major companies, there might be such a small population of people fitting this description that rather than randomly sampling from the population, you would work with every female CEO who would agree to participate. In this case, deliberately creating a sample in which each member has the specific experience or characteristic is a more useful approach.

SNOWBALL SAMPLING

Snowball sampling is another nonprobability technique for recruiting participants. This technique uses study participants' networks to expand the sample. Once a group of people is identified, they are then asked to recruit or refer other people they know. If you find 10 participants originally and each person refers 2 people and those people refer another 2 people, your sample has expanded dramatically to 70 participants. You can see the effect snowball sampling can have on sample size in figure 6.2. The example of recruiting female CEOs

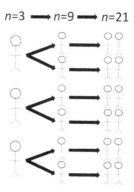

FIGURE 6.2 Snowball sampling

For a snowball sample, you select three individuals who then each refer two additional individuals. Each of the new individuals refers two additional individuals. Now your sample has gone from $n = 3$ to $n = 9$ to $n = 21$.

would lend itself well to snowball sampling. A female CEO may be more likely to be connected with other female CEOs and could encourage them to participate as well.

RANDOM SAMPLING

Random sampling, unlike convenience sampling, gives each individual in a population the same probability of being selected to participate. An equal probability of being selected eliminates systematic bias in the group of individuals who are asked to participate.

We will discuss several types of random sampling: simple random sampling, stratified sampling, and cluster sampling. There are other types of random sampling researchers can choose from, but those are beyond the scope of this book.

SIMPLE RANDOM SAMPLING

The key idea for a simple random sample is that each person has an equal chance of being selected. The simplest form of this type of sampling is to put the names of all potential participants on slips of paper, mix them up, and draw enough names for the sample. There are also easy ways of randomizing individuals using computer programs and random-number generators.

STRATIFIED RANDOM SAMPLING

Stratified random sampling builds on simple random sampling, but instead of drawing from the whole sample, the sample is first divided into groups based on important characteristics. Participants are then drawn randomly from those smaller groups or "strata."

For example, if you want to ensure that you are accurately representing the racial makeup of a community, you can create strata consisting of racial/ethnic groups, such as white, black or African American, Hispanic or Latino, Asian, American Indian, and Pacific Islander. If you know that 30 percent of the population in the community is African American, 20 percent is Latino, and 50 percent is white, then you can create strata that reflect those breakdowns and choose randomly within the strata. If your sample is to include 200 participants, then 60 will be African American, 40 will be Latino, and 100 will be white. By creating strata, you have ensured that your sample matches the racial/ethnic breakdown of the community while still randomizing the selection of any individual participant.

RANDOM CLUSTER SAMPLING

Random cluster sampling is similar to other types of random sampling discussed previously. The major difference is that instead of working with individuals, you sample groups or "clusters."

Random cluster samples could be useful if you are working in schools, which are clustered into classes. Instead of drawing a random sample of students from the six schools in your county, you could instead do a random sample of classes in your county. Now, instead of contacting each student to get information or provide an intervention, you might work with the teacher for each selected class and then provide the intervention to an entire class. Instead of working with a sample of 400 students, you are working with a sample of 20 classes, which together total 400 students.

Similarly, if you are interested in the effects of family therapy on participants, you might survey each individual participant or you could do a random cluster sample of the participating households. Instead of randomly sampling members of each participating family, you would randomly sample whole families and test every member of the selected families. Instead of working with a sample of 60 individuals, you are working with a sample of 15 households.

RANDOM ASSIGNMENT AND CAUSALITY

Now that you are familiar with nonprobability and random sampling, we can go a step further to explain why random sampling is superior (when possible) to nonprobability sampling. All sampling is concerned with representativeness and confounding factors. Confounding factors are those factors that affect both the dependent *and* independent variables, often leading to spurious associations.

Random samples have several benefits:

- Random samples eliminate, or at least randomly distribute, any confounding variables so they will not skew your results.
- Random samples, unlike convenience samples, can generate causal relationships.

When using a nonrandom sample, accounting for and addressing confounding variables is difficult, so you should be hesitant to draw causal conclusions from the results of nonrandom samples.

Random Sampling Versus Randomization

Random *selection* and random *assignment* are commonly confused or used interchangeably, but they are not the same. Random selection (also called random sampling) deals with the way participants are selected from a population. Random assignment, on the other hand, is part of an experimental design in which participants are randomly assigned to a treatment group or a group that does not receive treatment, called a control group.

Random sampling ensures that your sample is representative of the population you are interested in, so conclusions can be generalized to a larger population. Random assignment takes place following the selection of participants. Any given study can use both random sampling and randomization, random sampling without randomization, randomization without random sampling, or none of these.

Imagine you want to study the effectiveness of an intervention to improve parenting skills. You are interested in the population of parents of children at a local elementary school. If you used a random sampling method to create your sample, you would ensure that each set of parents had an equal chance of being chosen. By randomly selecting parents, you hope to select a group that represents the whole population of parents.

Then, if you also wanted to include a randomized design to test your parenting intervention, you would randomly assign each set of parents either to receive the intervention or to act as a control group by continuing as they had been without receiving the intervention. You will learn more about randomized control trials (RCTs) in later coursework, but for the purposes of this book, all you need to know is that the randomization of participants into treatment and control groups follows and is separate from random sampling. Strong studies will use both, but doing so is not necessary.

WHAT IS SAMPLING ERROR?

Sampling error is always present, even if you are using a type of random sampling. Sampling error measures the ways the sample you have selected does not match the population it was taken from, or the degree of misrepresentation in your sample.

If you cannot avoid sampling error, why bother with random sampling?

- Random sampling creates less sampling error than using nonrandom samples, even though it does not eliminate error. When using large sample sizes, the error in random samples can be small.
- Inferential statistics can capture how much error exists in random samples, so you are aware of the level and can determine if it is acceptable.

WHY IS A SAMPLE'S SIZE IMPORTANT?

You want to test an intervention and know you will select a sample, but how big a sample is big enough? You are working with resource constraints, so will a sample of 10 participants be sufficient, or do you need 100 or 1,000? Sample size (n) is the number of participants in a study. Carefully choosing a sample size, or critically reviewing the size of a sample in a research study, is necessary for two reasons:

1. The size of the sample influences the precision of estimates.
2. The size of the sample affects your ability to draw conclusions and find statistically significant results.

To use an example, we might compare the health outcomes of children whose parents have received Supplemental Nutrition Assistance Program (SNAP) benefits, often called food stamps. You are unable do checkups on every child who received food stamps, so you create a sample. The results will be more precise—more likely to represent the whole population—if the sample is 100 children instead of 50 children, and even more so with a sample of 1,000 children instead of 100 children.

The larger the anticipated difference you are trying to study in the population, the smaller the sample size can be. To pick up slight improvements in overall health and functioning of children, you must have a large sample, but if you are testing a medication you believe will make a big difference in the health of those who take it, then a smaller sample may be sufficient. Similarly, if you wanted to estimate the incidence of substance abuse among college students and took a sample of 20 students, then you might not find anyone using drugs or alcohol in unhealthy quantities. Substance abuse is sufficiently rare that 20 students might not be enough to identify this problem. If you took a sample of 500 students, you would be more likely to find a more precise measurement of the level of substance abuse in the population.

WHAT IS THE STANDARD ERROR OF THE MEAN AND HOW DO I USE IT?

You will remember from earlier chapters that the standard deviation measures the dispersion of data in a normal distribution. The standard error of the mean measures the accuracy of our estimate of the population mean based on the idea of taking many samples, finding their sample means, and then finding the dispersion of those sample means. The standard error is the standard deviation of all of these theoretical sample means. The standard error of the mean is used to make inferences about data from a sample to a population. This concept may not intuitively make sense. Consider the following example.

Imagine you are working with the population of middle school students (N) in public school in the United States. You would like each student to complete a measure to determine their aggression and experience of bullying other students. Unfortunately, you do not have the resources to work with every middle school student. Instead, you take a random sample of 100 individuals (n), and find the mean score for their experience of bullying based on your measure.

Would this mean match the mean of the larger population? Probably not. In fact, if you took 50 different samples of $n = 100$ out of the population, you would get a variety of means both above and below the true population mean.

CENTRAL LIMIT THEOREM

If you took the means of all 50 samples and created a distribution, the central limit theorem says that as long as the sample size is reasonably large, then the distribution of means is normal. Your distribution of means would share the characteristics you previously learned about normal distributions. The mean of the sample means is an unbiased estimate of the population mean. As the sample size gets larger, it approaches a normal distribution and the true population mean.

If you only have one sample rather than 50, how do you find the standard error of the mean?

$$Standard\ Error\ of\ the\ Mean = \frac{s}{\sqrt{n}}$$

Where

s = Standard deviation of the sample

n = Sample size

Consider the following example: You are reviewing student surveys and find that on a measure asking about the

number of times in the past week the student teased someone to make them angry (a variable of interest in determining aggression and bullying), the results were:

$n = 100$

$M = 8$

$s = 5$

Now use these scores to calculate the standard error of the
mean:

$$Standard\ Error\ of\ the\ Mean = \frac{s}{\sqrt{n}}$$

$$= \frac{5}{\sqrt{100}}$$

$$= \frac{5}{10}$$

$$= 0.5$$

The same rules you learned about standard deviation apply
to the standard error of the mean. The standard error of the
mean is a type of standard deviation, but for comparing your
sample mean to the overall population mean. About 68 percent of cases will fall within 1 standard deviation unit of the
mean. The standard error is equal to 0.5, so 68 percent of all
sample means will fall within 1 unit of the true population
mean. Therefore, a reliable estimate of the true population
mean is between 7.5 (8−0.5) and 8.5 (8+0.5).

You can increase your confidence by calculating two
standard deviations from the mean to get a 95 percent
confidence level. You can be 95 percent confident that the
true population mean is between 7 and 9 instances. These

ranges create a confidence interval for the true population mean for your variable of interest—the number of times a student teased someone to make them angry. You will see confidence intervals like this reported in most academic literature.

Usually, the bigger the sample, the smaller the standard error. That is because the bigger the sample, the more information is available to estimate the characteristic or variable of interest. This becomes clear if you examine the effects of increasing the sample size. If you quadruple the sample size, you cut the standard error in half.

Using the previous example, if instead of working with a sample of 100, consider the effect of using a sample of 400. Assuming the sample mean and standard deviation remain 8 and 5, respectively, for the larger sample, we can recalculate the confidence interval for our population mean as follows:

$$Standard\ Error\ of\ the\ Mean = \frac{s}{\sqrt{n}}$$

$$= \frac{5}{\sqrt{400}}$$

$$= \frac{5}{20}$$

$$= 0.25$$

Increasing the sample size has reduced the standard error. With this larger sample, a 95 percent confidence interval falls between 7.5 (−2 SD) and 8.5 (+2 SD) instances, instead of between 7 and 9.

KEY TAKEAWAYS

- Random sampling creates unbiased samples.
- Having a large enough sample size can improve your ability to find differences or results that can be extrapolated to the entire population.
- The less common the trait or characteristic you are trying to identify, the larger the sample should be.
- The standard error of the mean is a type of standard deviation that creates a confidence interval for the true population mean.

CHECK YOUR UNDERSTANDING

1. What type of sampling limits the risk of biased samples the most?
2. What type of sampling method is most likely being used in the following scenarios:
   a. You draw a sample from mothers who respond to your advertisement for parenting classes.
   b. You draw a sample of households within a school district.
   c. You draw a sample of clients who are undergoing treatment for depression with representation of men and women proportionate to the number of men and women receiving counseling.
3. You want to create a stratified random sample of 350 individuals when the breakdown of ages of people participating in a drug treatment program is as follows:

42 percent ages 16–25, 30 percent ages 26–40, and 28 percent ages 41–65. How many people should be selected from each age group?

4. True or False: The more common a trait or characteristic is, the larger the sample you will need to identify it.

5. If you have a sample of 150 and find a sample mean of 30 and a standard deviation of 5, find the standard error of the mean and define the 95 percent confidence interval.

7

WHAT WORKS?

Hypothesis Testing and Inferential Statistics

Hypothesis testing generates new knowledge. The human brain is constantly trying to find connections and draw conclusions about the world around us. These conclusions become ideas, hunches, or gut feelings that we believe are true about the world. You can operate in many parts of life solely by using these ideas or hunches, but as a social worker you want to use evidence-based practices. Rigorously testing your ideas about how the world works is an important way to ensure that your judgment, preconceptions, and biases are not infiltrating your work. Inferential statistics are a tool to test ideas—or hypotheses, in the jargon of statistics—to determine if the differences or relationships are due to chance or to the treatment being tested.

This chapter and the one that follows unpack the process of making hypotheses explicit and testing them for statistical significance.

Throughout your career, you will be introduced to literature and media that claim to have found significant results that should affect the way you practice. You will be a critical consumer of information if you understand what these claims mean and what they can and cannot tell you. These chapters provide the foundation for understanding how tests of statistical significance are done, and their limitations.

LEARNING OBJECTIVES

By the end of this chapter, you should understand the following concepts:

- How to create a hypothesis
- The difference between Type I and Type II errors in hypothesis testing
- How to use a t-test
- How the p-value is used to interpret results
- How to calculate effect size
- How to use effect size in addition to significance tests

WHAT IS A HYPOTHESIS?

A hypothesis begins as a question about the world that forms the basis of a theory to be tested. You can think about a hypothesis as "an educated guess." Anytime you observe the world, you look for relationships and try to make sense of what you are seeing. Hypotheses are a way to make explicit the ideas you have about how any given relationship works. They allow you to rigorously test your educated guesses.

When doing research, you start by assuming no relationship exists between the variables you are studying. You seek to prove this assumption incorrect, and you use statistical tests to quantify the likelihood that the relationship occurred by chance.

Imagine observing that when you offer childcare for attendees at a community meeting, more people show up for the event. You might think that the opportunity to bring their children and have someone to watch them allowed more people to come. That might be enough for you to start offering childcare at your next community meeting, but maybe the change in attendance just occurred by random chance. Maybe what drove the change was that you had the meeting on a Monday instead of a Friday and the timing worked better for people. Maybe your last meeting conflicted with an event at the local school. Maybe it was raining. Maybe parents decided tonight was a better night than other nights. You cannot know if childcare drove the increased turnout unless you test your hypothesis.

In any given inferential test, there are two hypotheses at play:

1. Null hypothesis
2. Alternative hypothesis

NULL HYPOTHESIS

The null hypothesis (expressed mathematically as H_0) represents the possibility that there is no significant difference between the populations you are interested in. The null hypothesis argues that any differences are due to error or chance, or that the two groups are the same. This would mean that there is no difference in turnout for your event whether you offer childcare or not. Any variation is either random or linked to another factor.

ALTERNATIVE HYPOTHESIS

The alternative hypothesis (expressed mathematically as H_a) represents your assumption that the intervention made a difference. The alternative hypothesis is your expectation about how the independent variable affects the dependent variable. Your alternative hypothesis is that more people attend community meetings when childcare is offered.

The null hypothesis is a check on your assumption. It represents the possibility that, even after the intervention, there is no difference between the group that received the intervention and the group that did not.

The null and alternative hypotheses are structured like this:

H_0: There is no difference between the group that received the intervention and the one that did not.

H_a: There is a difference between the group that received the intervention and the one that did not, and the difference is due to the independent variable (the intervention).

Here is another example:

H_0: $M_1 = M_2$ (The null hypothesis is that the first mean is equal to the second.)

$H_a: M_1 \neq M_2$ (The alternative hypothesis is that the first mean is not equal to the second.)

The first equation indicates that the mean for the first group is the same as the mean for the second group; there is no difference between the groups. This is the null hypothesis. The second indicates that the mean for the first group differs from the mean for the second group. This is the alternative hypothesis.

NONDIRECTIONAL ALTERNATIVE HYPOTHESIS

Stating that there is a difference makes this alternative hypothesis a nondirectional alternative hypothesis. The hypothesis in this case is that there is a difference, but the direction is not specified. An example would be "Parental engagement affects child behavior." This hypothesis does not venture a guess about whether parental engagement will improve child behavior or worsen child behavior, but it asserts that there will be a difference.

DIRECTIONAL ALTERNATIVE HYPOTHESIS

A directional alternative hypothesis goes a step further. If the evidence or your experience makes you confident in the direction of a relationship, then you can incorporate that into a hypothesis. "Providing childcare *improves* attendance" is a directional hypothesis, as is "Parental engagement *improves* child behavior."

CONSIDERING THE MEANS

As we discussed in chapter 4, the mean of a dataset can provide quick, useful information about groups you are comparing. You are more likely to find a statistically significant difference and reject the null hypothesis if the means of the groups are very different. Of the two groups shown in table 7.1, without further testing, which one is more likely to result in rejecting the null hypothesis?

Without any additional information, you might guess that the first experiment makes rejecting the null hypothesis more likely. The means in experiment 1 appear much more different than those in experiment 2. You would assume that there is less overlap between those distributions compared to the second set of distributions, even without having any other information.

Using figure 7.1, you can see by looking at the two distributions on a graph that the overlap in the second pair is greater than the overlap in the first. You can think of the shaded area as the area where you could not differentiate a person who was part of sample A from a person who was part of sample B. The larger that area, the more difficult it is to determine if there are significant differences between the

Table 7.1 Comparing Groups

Experiment 1: Sample A		Experiment 1: Sample B	
Mean = 15	SD = 5	Mean = 40	SD = 10
Experiment 2: Sample A		Experiment 2: Sample B	
Mean = 10	SD = 2	Mean = 11	SD = 1

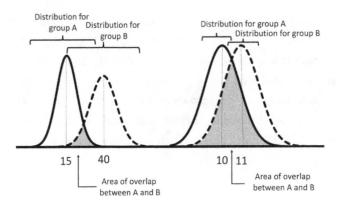

FIGURE 7.1 Using distributions to see group differences

Two sets of distributions are graphed. Each set includes two curves that graph the data for two groups. In the first set, there is a very small area where the two curves overlap. In the second set, the curves have a much large area of overlap. Telling the difference between the two groups where the distributions have a lot of overlap would be more difficult than telling the difference between the groups with only a small area of overlap.

two groups. Comparing distributions using the means and standard deviations gives you a sense of whether your inferential test will return a significant result.

HOW DO I TEST A HYPOTHESIS?

Now that you understand how to make your assumption explicit by identifying a hypothesis, you can test that hypothesis. The goal of inferential statistics is to establish a level of confidence that a difference you observe is due to the independent variable you are testing.

In figure 7.1, the first pair of distributions has little overlap, which is promising for finding a statistically significant result. Little overlap is not sufficient though. You must to do an inferential test.

This chapter will introduce the t-test, a test for two groups. The following chapter will build on that concept with ANOVA and chi-square tests, which are used if there are three or more groups.

WHAT IS A T-TEST?

As a professional, you will want to know whether interventions you deliver have the desired effects. To do this, you first identify a group of people who could benefit from the intervention. These may be your clients, community members, or some other group. From there, you develop a test for your intervention. The most common tests are to evaluate a group prior to providing the intervention and then again after receiving the intervention (a pre/posttest) or to give the intervention only to a subset of the larger group, so some members receive the intervention and others do not (experimental design). In either of these situations, you are focusing on only two groups, so the t-test is the most useful option in your statistics toolkit.

A t-test is used to determine whether there is a statistically significant difference between two groups. There are two kinds of t-tests (table 7.2):

1. Dependent, or paired sample
2. Independent

Table 7.2 T-Test Matrix

Dependent t-Test	Independent t-Test
A t-test for dependent means is used when a single group of subjects is being studied under two conditions—for example, evaluating the same subjects before an intervention (pre) and after an intervention (post).	The independent groups t-test is used to evaluate whether the means of two independent samples are equal—for example, comparing the effectiveness of an intervention by comparing the mean for a treatment group (intervention received) and a control group (no intervention).
Use this test when:	Use this test when:
The same participants are being tested more than once.	Differences between two separate groups are examined.
There are two samples (before and after).	Participants are being tested only once.

HOW DO I INTERPRET A TEST STATISTIC?

Results for t-tests in academic literature will look something like this:

$$t = 2.04, df = 30, p < .05$$

Unless you are doing research, interpreting the results of t-tests is more important than calculating a t-value. We do not cover the calculation for finding a t-value, but the results from a t-test break down into three distinct pieces of information, and you should understand how to interpret these results.

1. $t = 2.04$: The t-value is a test statistic, which is a standardized value calculated from your data, but not in the same units as your measurements. While knowing $t = 2.04$ may not tell you much, knowing that a t-test was done tells you that the study had two groups—either two samples from the same groups (pre/post) or two independent groups.

2. $df = 30$: The notation *df* refers to degrees of freedom. For t-tests, $df = n - 1$. If you remember from previous chapters that n is the notation for sample size, the degrees of freedom are one less than the sample size. If you know the degrees of freedom, you also know the size of the sample.

3. $p < .05$: To know if there was a statistically significant result, you need to understand the p-value. You will learn in the next section that the most common threshold for statistical significance is $p < .05$. These results meet that threshold, so the results are statistically significant.

Consider if, instead, you see results like these:

$$t = 1.7, df = 24, p < .10$$

1. $t = 1.7$: A t-test was done, so you are dealing with only two groups—either two samples from the same groups (pre/post) or two independent groups.

2. $df = 24$: The sample size was $n = 25$.

3. $p < .10$: The most common level for statistical significance is $p < .05$. These results do not meet that threshold, so they are not statistically significant.

WHAT IS STATISTICAL SIGNIFICANCE?

Statistical significance is a key concept for consuming research findings and understanding the limitations of "knowing" based on statistical tests. Statistical significance is the probability that a value has a certain level of precision.

P-VALUE

We describe statistical significance with something called a p-value. The p-value can also be referred to using the Greek symbol alpha (α). The most commonly used threshold for statistical significance is $p < .05$.

A p-value, or significance level, of $p < .05$ indicates less than a 5 percent chance of seeing the results you found if the null hypothesis is true. If there is truly no difference between the two groups, then there is less than a 5 percent risk that these results would occur by chance. Put another way, a 5 percent significance level means that there is a 5 percent risk of rejecting the null hypothesis when it is true. (This is called a Type I error; you will learn about error in the next section.)

Prior to conducting an inferential test, the p or alpha (α) level must be set to determine the level of risk that is acceptable for rejecting or accepting the null hypothesis. The alpha level is most commonly set at $p = .05$, but it could be set higher or lower based on the appetite for risk in a given situation. You could imagine that in a scenario where the treatment could cause harm or the side effects might be severe, your appetite for risk would be lower, so a p-value of $p = .01$ would be more appropriate.

Consider a situation in which a teenager is tested for and diagnosed with a severe mental illness. This teenager will now be prescribed medications that can have serious side effects and will have to face potential stigma from this diagnosis. Would you be willing to accept a 5 percent risk that the test generated a false positive and the teenager does not have the diagnosed condition? Would a 1 percent chance be more acceptable? When the consequences are severe, you accept less risk. You use p-values to set the acceptable level of risk.

Statistical Significance in Political Polling

Statistical significance is regularly mentioned in the news. For example, during political campaigns, the media often report the results of public opinion polling in the form "Candidate A has the support of 52 percent of the electorate, with a 4 percent margin of error." Given that most polling uses the standard alpha (α) level of $p = .05$, this means that there is a 95 percent chance that the true rate of support among the entire population for candidate A is between 48 and 56. When the next week the media report a "fall" in support for candidate A to only 49 percent (with the same margin of error), all that means is that there is now a 95 percent chance that the true rate of support among the entire population for candidate A is between 45 and 53. Even though the media reported a "drop in support," in reality candidate A's support may have held steady at anywhere between 48 and 53 (figure 7.2).

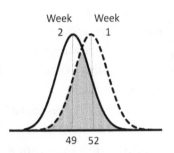

FIGURE 7.2 Distributions for support of a candidate over two weeks

The distributions representing support of a candidate over two weeks have a large area of overlap, which means that the candidate's support level could have been the same despite being reported as having declined.

If a test results in a p-value that is equal to or less than the alpha (α), then reject the null hypothesis (thus accepting the alternate hypothesis—your "educated guess"). If the result is greater than the α level, then you cannot reject the null hypothesis. If you cannot reject the null hypothesis, then there is not a statistically significant difference between the groups.

Remember that if a test does not reach the desired α level, you do not know that the intervention failed. The null hypothesis may not be true, but the sample data used in the calculation did not provide sufficient evidence to reject it. Similarly, a p-value of .05 does not mean that you have proved the alternative hypothesis. Even if the null hypothesis were true, there would still be a 5 percent chance of getting your result. If you were so convinced of the relationship that you kept testing for it, in 1 out of every 20 tests, you would be able to get a result where $p < .05$. Remember that each time you see a positive result reported in research literature, you may not see hundreds of attempts to test the same thing that did not find significant results.

Another risk is adhering too closely to the standard of $p = .05$. If a study found that the results of an intervention were significant to $p < .06$, that result would not reach the α level of $p < .05$, but it might still be promising enough to continue testing the intervention. The strict focus on $p < .05$ can be an overly narrow way to indicate the success of an intervention. The focus on this "bright line" result in published academic research has had the unfortunate consequence of driving some researchers to manipulate data in ways they otherwise might not have to find $p < .05$. (This is called p-hacking; you can learn more about it in chapter 9.)

HOW DO I KNOW IF A SIGNIFICANT RESULT IS MEANINGFUL?

Statistical significance does not always translate into meaningful differences that nonstatisticians appreciate. A "significant" result in statistics refers to solely the p-value, even though that use does not necessarily match the colloquial use of the word.

A small p-value does not necessarily ensure a larger or more important effect, and a larger p-value does not mean the results are unimportant or prove that the intervention does not work. With a large enough sample size, any effect, no matter how tiny, can produce a small p-value, and with a small sample or imprecise measurements, even an intervention that has a large effect may result in a nonsignificant p-value.

A study may be statistically significant but not meaningful. If a study found statistically significant results that extracurricular activities for teenagers lowered their use of alcohol, administrators would want to fund additional activities. However, if the statistically significant result showed that extracurricular activities lowered alcohol consumption by an average of only 0.5 drinks per week, then the practical implications may be limited. Schools may not be willing to spend more money encouraging students to participate in extracurricular activities or creating new clubs or sports teams to lower alcohol consumption by only half a drink a week if reducing alcohol consumption is their primary goal.

Similarly, if a study found statistically significant results that a job training program placed participants in jobs but that they held those jobs for less than two months, then the practical implications may be limited. The state may not be willing to spend more money on job training programs if they do not lead to long-term employment.

In each case, the results were statistically significant, but the implications for practice were not meaningful.

Return to the previous examples of t-test results:

$$t = 2.04, df = 30, p < .05 \quad \text{or} \quad t = 1.7, df = 24, p < .10$$

You now know that the commonly accepted level of risk is .05. When $p < .05$, you have sufficient confidence that there is a difference between the groups being examined.

At $p < .10$, you have not reached a sufficient level of confidence that the difference is produced by the intervention rather than by chance.

Using a t-Test in Practice

A city's Department of Human Services plans to launch a new flexible rent-subsidy pilot to reduce the number of families who become homeless and need shelter provided by the city. The subsidy is designed to help low-income families stay in housing despite short-term fluctuations in their income. This flexible subsidy could allow them to adjust for shifting or unstable hours at work or unexpected costs like flat tires or medical bills.

There are not enough funds to serve every eligible family, so the city randomly selects families to receive the subsidy and creates a waiting list. They can then compare the families who receive the subsidy ($n = 138$) to those who are still on the waiting list ($n = 234$) to see if there is a difference between the two groups in the average amount spent on social services (table 7.3).

There are two groups, the treatment and control group, which means that an independent t-test is the most appropriate test to determine if there is a difference in the amount spent on

Table 7.3 Mean Spending for Families in Treatment and Control Groups

	Received Subsidy	On the Waiting List
Mean spending per family during program year	$9,329	$13,321

---

social services for families at risk of homelessness. After completing a t-test, the city staff found the following results:

$$t = -12.46 \text{ and } p < .0001$$

A p-value of $< .0001$ is *extremely* small. This p-value indicates that there is only a 1 in 10,000 chance that these results are due to chance or that they represent a false positive. Given this result, the staff feel confident that the flexible subsidy has lowered the overall cost of supporting families, and they can use this information to advocate for expanding the program in the next year.

WHAT DO ERRORS TELL ME ABOUT MY RESULTS?

When you think about testing hypotheses, you may think that the alternative hypothesis (your educated guess) will either be rejected or not. Unfortunately, since you are never testing the entire population, determining if your result is valid is more complicated than that. For example, there is some chance that you will find no difference between the group that received the intervention and the one that did not, when in reality there *was* a difference. Alternatively, your test might find a difference between the two groups, when in reality there was *not* a difference.

TYPE I ERROR

Type I errors (α) occur when you conclude there is a difference when there is not (table 7.4). It is a false positive finding. If you

Table 7.4 Analyzing Hypotheses

	H_0 is True	H_0 is False
Reject H_0	Type I error (false positive)	Finding reflects reality
Do not reject H_0	Finding reflects reality	Type II error (false negative)

are testing an antidepressant and find that the people who took the medication have lower levels of depression, but really the difference was just due to chance, then that is a Type I error.

TYPE II ERROR

Type II errors (β) occur when you do not find a difference that exists. It is a false negative finding. If you found that the antidepressant did not make a difference when it actually lowered levels of depression, you have made a Type II error.

You cannot completely eliminate the risk of a Type I or Type II error when conducting tests, but you should understand the risk of each type of error and its implications. Calculating the precise risk of error is beyond the scope of this book. For most practitioners, it is sufficient to understand the implications of either a Type I or Type II error and know that there is always some risk involved.

Error in Practice

Imagine you are a counselor at a high school who is concerned about an increase in the number of teenage suicides. You want to help mediate this risk with your students. Your hypothesis is that a crisis intervention you designed will help your students, but you must test your hypothesis to be certain.

The null hypothesis is that your intervention does not make a difference and that the risk is the same for a group that receives the intervention and a group that does not. The alternative hypothesis is that your intervention reduces suicidal ideation—thinking about or planning to commit suicide.

If you conducted an experiment to test your intervention and found that the intervention was effective at reducing suicidal ideation, but in fact your results were just random chance, that is a Type I error. This result would lead to the belief that the intervention helps when it does not. Teenagers may receive a treatment that does not help them, possibly wasting time and resources or keeping them from an intervention that would be more effective. You obtained a false positive.

Instead, imagine you conducted an experiment and found that your intervention did not make a difference in students' suicidal ideation, when in fact it was making a difference. That result is a Type II error. This would lead to the belief that the intervention did not work when in fact it could reduce the risk of suicide. Here, teenagers are not receiving a treatment that could save lives.

If you are the counselor conducting the test, which risk is more acceptable, Type I or Type II? Do you continue testing an intervention that may not work, or do you set aside an intervention that may be helping but that you do not yet have statistical proof to back up?

Type II error can occur because a small sample size limits the power of the test. When you review literature, or are testing interventions yourself, keep the risk of Type II error in mind if you are working with only a few people. You will have trouble overcoming Type II error unless you can test the intervention with a larger group.

WHAT IS THE EFFECT SIZE?

Effect size is a simple way of quantifying the magnitude of the difference between two groups. Effect size emphasizes the size of the difference in terms of standard deviations, so the difference is more easily compared across groups.

The effect size is particularly valuable for quantifying the effectiveness of a particular intervention relative to some comparison. It allows you to move beyond the simplistic "Does the intervention work or not?" to the far more sophisticated "How well does the intervention work in a range of contexts?" Moreover, by placing the emphasis on the size of the effect rather than any statistical significance, you can more easily translate results into their practical implications.

HOW DO I CALCULATE THE EFFECT SIZE?

The effect size is calculated using Cohen's d. Cohen's d is a measure of effect size based on the difference between two means. Because Cohen's d uses the means for two groups, this measurement of effect size is only useful in conjunction with t-tests.

The effect size is calculated as follows:

$$\text{Cohen's } d = \frac{x_1 - x_2}{(SD_1 + SD_2)/2}$$

$$= \frac{\text{Mean of the experimental group} - \text{Mean of the control group}}{\text{Pooled standard deviation}}$$

You can evaluate the effect size using the following guidelines (figure 7.3). If Cohen's d is around 0.2, then the effect size is small. If it is around 0.5, then the effect size is considered medium. If the effect size is around 0.8, this is considered a large effect size. If the effect size is greater than 1, then that is a very large effect size.

When calculating Cohen's d, you may find a negative result. If x_1 in your equation is the experimental group and x_2 is the control group, then a negative effect size indicates

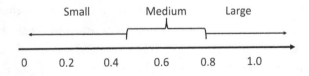

FIGURE 7.3 Measuring magnitude of effect size

A scale for measuring the magnitude of the effect size, ranging from 0 (no effect) to 1 or more (a large effect). In the middle is a range from about 0.5 to 0.8 where the effect size is considered medium.

that the effect was negative (rather than improving the condition, it caused deterioration, or rather than an increase, there was a decrease). In general, the sign of the effect size is not as important as the magnitude. However, you should always verify that the direction of the change matches your assumption.

Finding a small effect size does not mean that the treatment under consideration has no effect. Finding a small effect size means that the only way to identify the effect or difference is by using precise instruments with a large sample size. For large effect sizes, you may be able to see the difference between the two groups simply by observing them. Consider an effective antibiotic. If an antibiotic was given to one group of people suffering from an illness while the other group received a placebo, you should be able to tell who received the antibiotic by looking at whose symptoms have ceased. This is an example of a very large effect size. You can observe the difference without careful testing (though you should still conduct tests!).

It should make sense that if Cohen's d is larger than 1.0, it is a very large effect size. Effect size indicates how many standard deviations the mean of the experimental group is from the mean of the control group. If Cohen's d is equal to 1, then there is a full standard deviation between the means. You will remember from chapter 4 that nearly all scores fall between $+/-3$ standard deviations from the mean, and that 68 percent of scores fall between $+/-1$ standard deviation from the mean. Finding more than 1 standard deviation between the means is a substantial difference.

UNDERSTANDING EFFECT SIZE USING DISTRIBUTIONS

Using graphical representations can help clarify the meaning of the effect size. The goal of the effect size is to standardize the size of a difference between two means using the variance between the two distributions.

Start by considering the distribution in figure 7.4.

You can see that the means are close and the overlap is large. The distributions are also flat, which indicates larger standard deviations. What does this tell you about the effect size?

First, the large amount of overlap between the two distributions indicates that identifying whether a person was in the treatment or control group would be difficult. The differences would not be clear. Second, the large standard

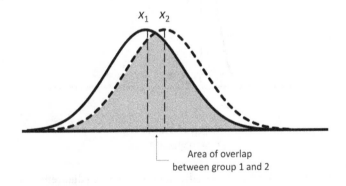

FIGURE 7.4 **Understanding distributions with a small effect size**

Two distributions with means that are close together and large standard deviations have a large amount of overlap. In this situation, you would assume the effect size is small.

deviation (the distributions are more flat than peaked) means that the denominator of the effect size calculation will be larger and the resulting Cohen's *d* will be smaller.

Compare the distributions in figure 7.4 to the distributions in figure 7.5.

The means in figure 7.5 appear to be more different. There is little overlap between the two distributions, but they also appear to have large standard deviations. The denominator of the effect size calculation will be large, and the resulting Cohen's *d* will be small, though not as small as in the first set

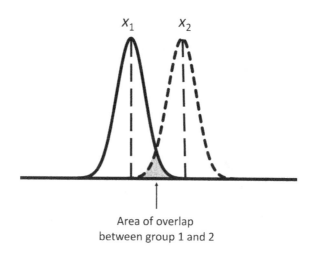

Area of overlap
between group 1 and 2

FIGURE 7.5 Understanding distributions with a medium effect size

Two distributions with means that are not close together and large standard deviations have a smaller amount of overlap. In this situation, you would assume the effect size is medium.

of distributions because the overlap between the two distributions is smaller.

Finally, compare the distributions in figure 7.4 and 7.5 to the distribution in figure 7.6.

The means in figure 7.6 appear to be more similar, like those in figure 7.4. But the distributions are quite peaked, indicating smaller standard deviations, so there is little overlap between the two distributions. These distributions will have a larger effect size than the distributions in figure 7.4.

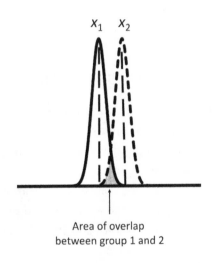

Area of overlap
between group 1 and 2

FIGURE 7.6 Understanding distributions with a large effect size

Two distributions with means that are close together and small standard deviations have a small amount of overlap. In this situation, you would assume the effect size is large.

KEY TAKEAWAYS

- T-tests tests allow you to determine if there is a difference between two groups.
- The significance level is the amount of risk you are willing to accept that you rejected the null hypothesis, or said there was a difference between groups, when there was no difference.
- Not all statistically significant results have meaningful practical implications.
- If Cohen's d is around 0.2, it is considered small. If it is around 0.5, it is considered medium. If it is around or above 0.8, then it considered a large effect size.

CHECK YOUR UNDERSTANDING

1. You manage an agency that provides tutoring services. You are interested in starting a new literacy program for clients at your agency. You serve many people at your agency, but logistically you think you can only study the effect of the new program with 60 people. You randomly assign those 60 people so that 30 people receive services as usual and 30 people participate in your new literacy program. The results are shown in table 7.5.

   a. What are the null and alternative hypotheses?
   b. Which t-test should you use?
   c. What significance level would you set?

Table 7.5 Test Scores for an Experimental Literacy Program

	Mean Score on Standardized Reading Test (Out of 200)	Standard Deviation
Services as usual	150	29
Literacy program	175	35

2. Identify if each of the following situations is an example of an independent or a dependent t-test.

   a. You want to know if there is a difference in stress level between a group that did not participate in a meditation training workshop and a group that did.

   b. You test older adults' stability while walking before and after completing a falls-prevention and physical activity program.

   c. You gauge whether or not a campaign against bullying changed student attitudes.

3. Identify if each of the following situations is an example of Type I or Type II error.

   a. You track stress levels for children who are taken into the foster care system, measuring their stress level when they are removed from the home, when they are in foster care, and once family reunification has occurred. Your results indicate that family reunification does not lower children's stress levels, but in reality reunification does lower stress levels.

   b. You are working with patients recently released from the hospital who need to monitor and manage their

Table 7.6 Scores for Experimental and Control Groups

	Mean	Standard Deviation
Experimental group	20	2
Control group	15	4

diabetes. You test a system of text-message reminders for when they should take their medicine and check their blood sugar. The results show that this intervention improved their management of the disease, but in reality the improvement was just random chance.

4. Which of the following represents a statistically significant result?

   a. $t = 1.350, df = 13, p < .08$
   b. $t = 2.074, df = 22, p < .025$
   c. $t = 1.108, df = 8, p < .15$

5. Calculate Cohen's d using the information in table 7.6.

6. Are the following effect sizes considered small, medium, or large?

   a. 0.8
   b. 1.5
   c. 0.3
   d. 0.6

7. True or False: A large effect size indicates a meaningful result.

8

WHEN TWO IS NOT ENOUGH

Testing with Multiple Groups

In the previous chapter, you learned about hypothesis testing and significance levels. In this chapter, you will build on this knowledge with two additional tests that you can use when you are analyzing more than two groups or when you do not have ratio-level data.

A t-test can analyze the difference between two groups, either independent or dependent groups. As discussed in the previous chapter, t-tests are useful when doing pre/post tests or when studying a single pair of treatment and control groups. What do you do when the samples you are working with are not so simple? What if you are comparing two different treatments to a control? What if the data you are able to collect are not ratio level? You will use either ANOVA tests or chi-square tests.

LEARNING OBJECTIVES

By the end of this chapter, you should understand the following concepts:

- How to use the ANOVA test
- How to use the chi-square test
- How to determine which test is appropriate for a given situation
- How to apply a social-justice lens to statistics

WHAT IS AN ANOVA TEST USED FOR?

The analysis of variance (ANOVA) test is similar to the t-test. Both are used to determine if there is a statistically significant difference between means. However, instead of analyzing just two means, ANOVA is used for several means. Like t-tests, ANOVA tests require the assumption that the distribution of your variables is normal.

ANOVA and t-tests are closely related. A t-test is the same as an ANOVA for two groups. If you do an ANOVA test on two groups, the result is the same as squaring the result of a t-test.

ANOVA tests are used to determine if a statistically significant difference exists among three or more groups. There are two types of ANOVA tests (table 8.1):

1. One-way
2. Two-way

Consider an example in which a one-way ANOVA test is applied to three or more means. You are working in a clinic and have access to a new medication that can treat anxiety.

Table 8.1 Comparing One-Way and Two-Way ANOVA

One-way ANOVA	Two-way ANOVA
One-way ANOVA allows you to determine if a difference exists among three or more means. Sometimes this is called simple analysis of variance.	Two-way ANOVA allows us to evaluate the effect of two independent variables and the interaction between them. Sometimes this is called factorial design.
Use this test when:	Use this test when:
- There is one independent variable.	- There are two or more independent variables. - You want to know the effect of different factors.
Example:	Example:
Do SAT scores differ for low-, middle-, and high-income students? (three groups of interest but only one independent variable)	Do SAT scores differ for high school students based on income level and ethnicity? (two independent variables of interest—income level and ethnicity)

After speaking with some clients who have tried it, you hypothesize that a medium dosage of the medication works best. In order to confirm your theory, you randomly split a list of clients into three groups to gather data and check the significance of your findings. The first group receives 200 milligrams per dose, the second group receives 100 milligrams per dose, and the third group receives a placebo that contains no medication. For each client, you measure heart rate and cortisol levels in their blood as measures of physical response to anxiety. Since you have means for three groups (200 milligram dose, 100 milligram dose, and placebo), you cannot use a t-test, but you can use a one-way ANOVA test to determine if there is a statistically significant difference in anxiety based on the dosage received.

Now consider the use of two-way ANOVA. You would use a two-way ANOVA if, in addition to testing the dosage of the new antianxiety medication, you also wanted to test the effect of gender, studying male, female, and nonbinary results along with the different dosages.

HOW DO I INTERPRET A TEST STATISTIC?

When reviewing literature related to ANOVA, you will likely come across reports of results that look something like this:

$$F_{(3,59)} = 2.7581, p < .05$$

This result is from a one-way ANOVA. This textbook will not cover how to find the F statistic or the degrees of freedom, because you are unlikely to need these calculations in your practice. The results listed above break down into three distinct pieces of information:

1. $F = 2.7581$: F is a test statistic for ANOVA. While knowing that $F = 2.7581$ may not tell you much, just knowing that an ANOVA was done tells you that the study you are looking at involved more than two groups.

2. **3, 59**: These two values are the degrees of freedom (df). For ANOVA tests like this one, there are two values listed for the degrees of freedom. The first is the df for the between-groups variance ($df = k - 1$), and the second is the df for the within-groups variance ($df = N - k$), where k is the number of groups and N is the population size. In this example, you know that four groups were made up of 63 participants total.

3. $p < .05$: Knowing that $p < .05$ tells you that the results are statistically significant. The results from an ANOVA are not as straightforward as those from a t-test, though. You know there is a difference among the groups, but you don't know which group is driving the difference.

The F statistic cannot be negative. F has a limit of zero, which rarely occurs because an F of zero means that the values for the dependent variables between the groups being examined are exactly the same.

A significant result ($p < .05$) for an ANOVA reveals that there is at least one significant difference among the means, but it cannot tell you which of the groups or characteristics you are evaluating is responsible. To determine which group is driving the difference, an additional test must be done.

POST HOC TEST

The tests conducted after completing an ANOVA are called post hoc (Latin for "after this") tests. The idea behind all of these tests is that each group mean is compared to every other group mean, so every possible relationship is studied. These

Table 8.2 Two-Way ANOVA Results

Source	F	p
Variable 1	1.63	0.0153
Variable 2	4.64	0.014
Interaction ($V_1 \times V_2$)	21.12	0.198

additional tests are beyond the scope of this book, but each one results in a p-value that indicates whether that group is driving the significant difference.

The results from a two-way ANOVA are usually presented in a table that compares the different independent variables. The results of a two-way ANOVA would look something like table 8.2.

In table 8.2, you can see that the results are presented for each variable. These variables might be the dosage of a medication, the hours of therapy received, or some other characteristic of the intervention. You may be using a second variable of interest to examine the relationship with your first independent variable, such as gender, age, socioeconomic status, or some other characteristics of the population you are studying.

These results tell you that there is a statistically significant result for variable 1 and for variable 2 ($p < .05$) but that the interaction between the two is not significant. With one test, you have concluded that you can reject two of three null hypotheses. For variables 1 and 2, you can say there was a difference between the groups being tested and use post hoc tests to determine which group was driving the statistically significant results.

ANOVA in Practice

Imagine you are working for a community organization that wants to do a needs assessment to design programming for a five-year strategic plan. To do the needs assessment, you will survey people who live in the neighborhood your organization operates in about what issues are most important to them. You previously wrapped up an initiative focused on ensuring that community members had access to health insurance, and now you are considering three proposed priority areas for the next initiative.

1. School readiness: The elementary school in the neighborhood reports that children are not prepared when they enroll in kindergarten. Their lack of preparation is causing challenges for teachers and for students, who fall behind from an early age.
2. Food access: The neighborhood is a food desert with limited access to food, especially fresh fruits and vegetables.
3. Community beautification: There has been an increase in the amount of graffiti on the main street of the neighborhood, and the local park has not been properly maintained. There are also a few abandoned lots that are in serious disrepair.

Your organization only has the resources to focus on one of these initiatives, so the survey results will help you identify

Table 8.3 Mean Scores of Survey Respondents by Age and Interest Area

	Under 30	30–50	Over 50
School readiness	8	5	4
Food access	6	7	7
Community beautification	7	5	8

community interest. You ask community members to rank the importance of each initiative on a scale of 1 to 10 (table 8.3).

You have the results of your survey, and now you want to identify if a difference in priorities exists among groups within the community. You want to compare people under age 30, individuals between 30 and 50, and individuals over age 50.

To do that, you use a two-way ANOVA test to determine if there is a difference in responses for these three groups, using the mean score for each group on each initiative (table 8.4).

A number of conclusions can be drawn from these test results:

- There are statistically significant differences in responses based on the type of project being considered.
- There are statistically significant differences based on the age of the respondent.

Table 8.4 ANOVA Results

Source	F	p
Project	4.4	0.0153
Age	5.87	0.0042
Interaction (age × project)	12.47	<.0001

- There are statistically significant differences when considering the interaction between age and the project being considered.

Based on this information, you know that there were differences in preferences based on the project type and the age of respondents. The mean scores for each type of project varied significantly, and the mean ages of participants varied significantly by group. Most important, you know that there are differences in the project preference based on the age of the survey respondent. The interaction between project type and age refers to the relationship between the mean score for project preference and age. The interaction when these two factors are combined still produces a statistically significant result. Now you can do post hoc tests to determine which age groups preferred each project. Looking at the mean values in table 8.3, you may expect to find that because the score for community beautification was highest among the over-50 cohort and school readiness had the highest score in the under-30 cohort, these groups were most supportive of these projects, but you would not know for certain without completing the post hoc tests.

HOW DO I USE A CHI-SQUARE TEST?

The chi-square (χ^2) test is different from the other tests we have discussed previously in two important ways. First, it does not require an assumption that the data are normally distributed. Second, the data can be nominal or categorical.

As you will remember from previous chapters, nominal and categorical data do not allow for the computation of a mean or standard deviation. The best you can do is a frequency. If you are studying whether preferences for certain careers vary between men and women, you cannot get a mean score for gender or for the names of occupations. These nominal variables are not compatible with a t-test or ANOVA, but they are no problem for a chi-square test.

Chi-square can be used in two scenarios. The first, most common scenario is when testing the differences between two or more actual samples. The second is when testing the difference between an actual sample and a hypothetical or previously established distribution. You are more likely to use or see a chi-square test in the context of comparing nominal or categorical data from two or more actual samples.

While chi-square tests are done on variables that generate frequencies rather than means, the actual test is conducted using the number of occurrences and not the frequency as a percentage or proportion. If you were comparing a variable based on gender, you would not use the percentage of female participants (e.g., 40 percent) but the count of participants (e.g., 84 people).

The chi-square test is then used to measure the strength of the association between two variables (gender and profession, for example), finding the difference between observed and expected frequencies.

Chi-Square in Practice

Social workers in a community mental health center noticed that a major threat to the success of their clients was "no shows": patients made an appointment but did not show up, or patients received a referral for services but never scheduled their first appointment.

Clinicians noticed people who frequently missed appointments appeared to hold certain common misconceptions about therapy. Many of these concerned the pragmatics of therapy, such as scheduling and the availability of clinicians. Negative attitudes about therapy were also common, as were negative experiences with past episodes of therapy. Clinicians worked together to develop a list of the most common problems, and developed a one-session Engagement Group to address them. (Greeno et al. 2012)

Once the intervention was developed, two groups were established. Both groups consisted of "no shows"; the difference between the groups was that one was offered the Engagement Group intervention and the other was not. For each of these groups, the outcome being measured was treatment attendance over the following twenty weeks (table 8.5).

Table 8.5 Percent Starting Treatment After Missing Initial Assessment

	Not offered Engagement Group	Offered Engagement Group
n	38	31
Therapy attendance	16%	45%

The results were analyzed using a chi-square test.

$$\chi^2 = 7.16, p < .01$$

From the results, you can see that there was a statistically significant difference in therapy attendance for individuals who attended the engagement group ($p < .01$).

Identifying a promising intervention based on clinical experience will allow social workers to potentially lower the number of missed appointments, which can "undermine client outcomes, clinician morale, and clinic finances."

Now, all future clients will be offered these engagement groups. If the results of increasing engagement continue to hold, then over the next one thousand incoming clients, hundreds may receive needed treatment who otherwise would have remained "no shows" in the community health center records.

Insights gained from your practice as a clinician may be valuable to other social workers in your field. One way to easily communicate your experience is in the language of statistical analysis.

HOW DO I CHOOSE WHICH TEST TO USE?

Now that we have discussed t-tests, ANOVA, and chi-square, you can use the decision tree in figure 8.1 to select which test is appropriate in a given circumstance:

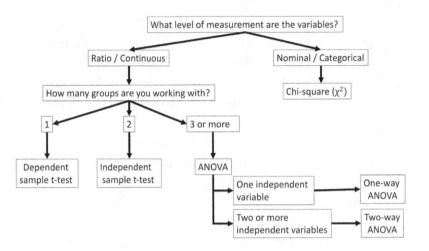

FIGURE 8.1 Decision tree for determining the appropriate inferential test

A decision tree, beginning with the level of measurement of the variables. For ratio/continuous variables, the number of groups determines the following step. If there is one group, you use a dependent t-test. If there are two groups, you use an independent t-test. If there are three or more groups, you use an ANOVA. If the ANOVA has one independent variable, you use a one-way ANOVA; if it has two or more independent variables, you use a two-way ANOVA. If the variable is nominal/categorical, you use a chi-square test.

SOCIAL JUSTICE AND INFERENTIAL STATISTICS

Now that you have learned how to use inferential statistics, consider ways you can put these new tools to use as a social worker. Regardless of the population you work with, using inferential tests or understanding them in academic literature can help ensure you are using evidence-based practices to provide the highest quality care available to your clients.

As a social worker, you can take these tools a step further to think critically about how you can use them to promote social justice. In social work practice, we pay particular attention to the needs and empowerment of vulnerable populations. This lens can be a valuable one to bring to statistics and the academic literature in our field.

Not every question is tested and not every group is represented in published studies. You can begin to incorporate a social justice framework in your use of statistics by considering what groups we know the most about. Whose experience do you see valued in scientific research? Are the samples used diverse? Are the questions asked relevant to pressing concerns of marginalized communities? Who benefits most from the data that are published? Whose values may be implicitly represented or excluded?

You can also take steps to remedy these disparities. Do you work with a population that is often underrepresented? Are they more diverse than the literature you find on the subject you care about? Do you work with people who are undocumented, who identify as LGBTQ, or who use drugs? If so, can you contribute to undoing some of the disparities in the information available about these groups? Can you share what you learn about your clients to pave the way for better practices in the future? Can you publish a study that tests the work you are doing? Can you partner with a university to make the process easier?

As a profession, social work is more likely to put you in a position to interact with underrepresented groups. By ensuring that evidence of what is effective for those groups exists, you are giving voice to their specific circumstances and prioritizing their needs rather than hoping they match up with the needs of a majority group.

Understanding inferential statistics and using these tools can make the work you do applicable on a much larger scale. Situating your work in the language of statistics makes the description of your work accessible to a larger audience who can use and build on your work. The work you will do is important; consider sharing it through the language and methods of statistics.

Keys for Using Statistics in Your Practice

When you are using academic literature to help determine how to best support your clients, remember to ask questions like these:

- Did the researchers account for all relevant variables?
- Did the researchers fail to capture information about underrepresented groups?
- Are there other factors the researchers did not study that may be causing the correlation they reported?
- Is a study's finding of a narrow improvement with high statistical significance enough to mean that a new intervention is worth the resources required to implement it, or just that it should be studied further?

When you are in clinical practice situations as a social worker, remember to collect data that can be effectively analyzed and to use statistics to your advantage.

- Advocate for data collection to be done in ways that include underrepresented groups, such as allowing for more than a binary choice when selecting gender or including people who are undocumented immigrants in studies of local residents.
- Use collected data and inferential statistical tests to show the significance of a new intervention you are recommending that your colleagues adopt.
- Help your team of social workers provide better care by identifying and spreading best practices based on data, not hunches.

As an advocate for your clients within your organization, within the community, or with elected officials, understand and apply statistics.

- Describe the scope of the problem you are addressing or the population you work with.
- Make the case that the intervention you are advocating for is effective.
- Understand and effectively respond to other stakeholders who use statistical analysis to support their perspective.
- Provide a reliable measure of how large an effect an investment of community resources is likely to have.

KEY TAKEAWAYS

- Use ANOVA tests when comparing the means of more than two groups or conditions.
- Use chi-square tests when comparing nominal or categorical variables.

CHECK YOUR UNDERSTANDING

1. Which inferential statistic test is appropriate in each of the following situations?
   a. You are doing a pre/post test with a group of older adults with a dementia diagnosis to determine if cognitive exercises have an effect on their level of impairment.
   b. You want to compare the outcomes on a depression inventory for two types of treatment: cognitive behavioral therapy and an approach that includes antidepressants. You have a control group that received neither treatment.
   c. By testing students at the beginning of the summer and at the end of the summer, you hope to prove that summer camp improves reading retention rates.
   d. You want to know if the types of jobs clients take after completing a job readiness training program vary by gender.

2. Table 8.6 reports the results from an academic study. What type of test was conducted?

Table 8.6

Source	F	p
Happiness	3.25	0.05
Treatment	19.69	0.001
Interaction (treatment × happiness)	1.32	0.21

3. A journal article reports the following:
   $\chi^2 = 21.026$, $df = 12$, $p < .05$
   Is this a statistically significant result?
4. How is an ANOVA test different from a t-test?

9

AN INTRODUCTION TO ADVANCED CONCEPTS

Over the previous eight chapters, you have learned many of the key concepts that you will use in your practice. Hopefully, this new knowledge has empowered you to think about the ways statistics contributes to improving your practice and helping you better serve your clients.

In addition to the key concepts already covered, this chapter will provide a brief introduction to some of the more advanced concepts that you might encounter. The details of these concepts are beyond the scope of this book and are generally the domain of statisticians, not social workers. Still, some exposure to these concepts is useful and can provide a spark for additional learning if the concepts interest you.

LEARNING OBJECTIVES

By the end of this chapter, you should understand the following concepts:

- What regression is
- How using a one- or two-tailed test affects tests
- What statistical models are
- What Bayesian statistics are
- What p-hacking is

REGRESSION

Regression is a tool that allows you to quantify a relationship between variables while also controlling for other factors. When you learned about correlations and saw scattergrams of data for two variables plotted, the line that best fit those data was created using regression analysis. This tool allows you to isolate the effect of one variable on another while holding other factors constant. If you wanted to know how participation in a religious community affects health outcomes like blood pressure or anxiety, then you would want to hold constant factors like income level, education level, age, and other health conditions to ensure that you were only seeing the effect of the variable of interest.

A common type of regression is linear regression. Linear regression fits a straight line to the data in a way that ensures that each point is as close as possible to the line, or the line is the "best fit." The line does not intersect every point, but it is the best description of all the points taken together to show a relationship.

In figure 9.1, you can see that a line has been fit to the data points. This line is created using regression analysis and the

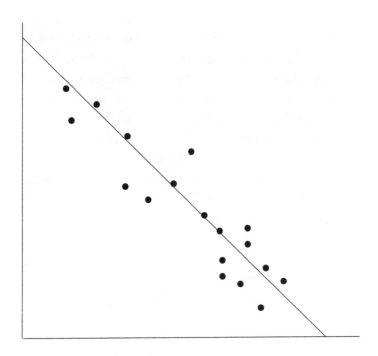

FIGURE 9.1 Linear regression

To graphs of linear regressions modeling the relationship between two variables.

equation $y = ax + b$, where y is the dependent variable, x is the independent variable, b is the slope of the line or how much the dependent variable changes for each unit of the independent variable, and a is the y-intercept (the value of y when x is zero).

Many studies you see that discuss relationships but are not randomized control trials use regression analysis. The key to successful regression analysis is choosing which variables should be isolated and how best to do so. If you overlook a key variable and do not control for it, your results may reflect a relationship that is not the one you believe you are studying. When using regression analysis, you are limited in the same ways as you are for any type of inferential statistics. You have selected data relevant to the question you are trying to answer, but those data only represent a certain group of people at a certain time. You still have to determine if the results can be applied to other populations.

When you come across a regression analysis in the literature, you should check for a few things before deciding whether to use this information in your practice.

1. Is the relationship linear? If the pattern created by the data points does not generally follow a straight line, then linear regression is not appropriate.
2. Are all important variables controlled for? If age is likely to have a big effect on any health outcomes of interest, does the study control for age? What about income? Are there other factors that could contribute to this relationship that have not been addressed?
3. Is the sample used in the analysis similar to the people you work with? The results of these analyses are only applicable to samples that are similar. If you work with children, a sample made up of adults is unlikely to be useful to you. If you work with people who live in cities, a sample of rural farmers is unlikely to be useful to you.
4. Remember that correlation is not causation. Regression analysis cannot tell you that one variable caused an effect in the other. You may find a statistically significant

relationship between two variables that have nothing to do with each other but happen to behave in similar ways. Beware of spurious correlations.

MORE ON HYPOTHESES: ONE- AND TWO-TAILED TESTS

Returning to the concept of hypothesis testing from chapter 7, you can further refine your practice by understanding the differences between one- and two-tailed tests.

For either a one- or two-tailed test, assume you are still using the significance level of .05. A two-tailed test distributes half of your alpha to testing the statistical significance in one direction and half to testing statistical significance in the other direction (figure 9.2). This means that each tail of the distribution uses an alpha of .025. A two-tailed test analyzes the possibility that a relationship exists, without predicting its direction. For example, it tests for the possibility that a treatment improved outcomes *or* worsened outcomes. Similarly, you could be interested in whether an intervention affected a family's earnings; a two-tailed test would test if incomes were either greater than or less than the value of the null hypothesis. With a two-tailed test, in order to be statistically significant, the results must be in either the top or the bottom 2.5 percent of the distribution, resulting in a p-value less than .05.

Alternatively, a one-tailed test distributes the alpha of .05 exclusively to one end of the distribution and does not

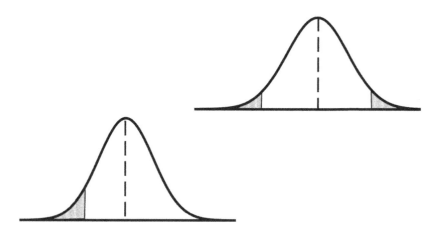

FIGURE 9.2 One- and two-tailed tests

A one-tailed test indicates a hypothesis that specifies whether the effect of a treatment or a relationship will be greater or less than the control. A two-tailed test is used for nondirectional hypotheses. For a one-tailed test, the area under the curve that represents $p < .05$ is situated at one end of the distribution, where the effect is expected to be found. For a two-tailed test, the area is split, with an area of $.025$ under each end of the curve.

test the other end of the distribution at all. If you wanted to know if an intervention increased family income, a one-tailed test would give you more power to detect the increase, but it would not test for a decrease at all. You are more likely to find a statistically significant result, but you risk missing results on the other end of the distribution. In some situations, missing an effect on the other end of the distribution can be a serious problem. Consider the possibility that you are interested in testing an antipsychotic medication. You want to maximize the chance of finding a statistically significant result for improved functioning on the medication, so you use a one-tailed test. In doing so, you can no longer find evidence that the medication is less effective than an existing drug or no treatment, whichever control you are using. Because this type of oversight is not acceptable in many situations, two-tailed tests are generally preferred. One-tailed tests should only be used when there is no risk or ethical concern in disregarding one direction of the effect.

P-HACKING: THE PRESSURE FOR STATISTICAL SIGNIFICANCE

In previous chapters, you have learned that the standard threshold for statistical significance is $p < .05$. This standard has been central to decisions about what studies are published and spread through the academic literature, but there is now a debate about its utility. A growing number of studies that reached the $p < .05$ threshold have not been replicable, calling into question their original validity. Additional studies have also found that there is a preponderance of published studies with results exactly equal to $p < .05$. Stunningly, about 90 percent of the papers published in academic journals documented positive findings where $p < .05$ (Silver 2012).

The problem with the struggle to find statistical significance is that researchers can consciously, or unconsciously, alter their results in such a way that they reach a statistically significant result and are able to publish a more interesting article than one that fails to reject the null hypothesis.

Suppose some researchers are considering the effect of income on mental health. They first consider income as all resources of the household (paychecks, food stamps, tax refunds, health insurance, and gift), and they do not find a statistically significant result. Then maybe they consider income to be only money coming in from paychecks. This time they do find a statistically significant result, and they publish this finding instead. In this case, the researchers can likely justify the change without using complicated calculations to achieve a statistically significant p-value (though that can also happen). The problem arises when, in the search for statistical significance, the researcher keeps trying until a statistically significant result is found. A disturbing number of published findings cannot be replicated when the experiment is conducted again by different researchers. This has led to calls to lower the p-value required for statistical significance or to abandon statistical significance in favor of effect size and the inclusion of descriptive statistics. One other emerging trend is prominent academic journals' actively promoting the publishing of results that fail to reach statistical significance, emphasizing that data from studies that are not statistically significant should also be considered as part of the body of literature.

For your practice, you should be aware that while the $p < .05$ level is a useful threshold and can be suggestive of interesting results, a study that finds this result does not necessarily mean you will get the same outcome if you repeat the intervention with the population you work with.

STATISTICAL MODELING

Statistical modeling at its simplest is a strategy for explaining the variation you see in the data you collect. The model is a way of analyzing the data and estimating the accuracy of the data for describing a larger population. Many modeling tools can be used, depending on the characteristics of the data. If the data you collect appear to be linear, approximately fitting a straight line, an appropriate model will be different than if your data appear to be curved, with observations that are higher in the middle of the distribution than at either end. The goal is to be able to use a model to predict values for unobserved relationships based on what you already know from observed data.

If you remember the discussion of scattergrams in chapter 5, you would graph the value of each observation and observe a linear positive relationship, a linear negative relationship, or a curvilinear relationship. You select an appropriate statistics model by observing these patterns in the data.

Once an appropriate statistical model is selected, the purpose of the model is to extrapolate from the observed data to unobserved data about a larger population.

This textbook will not prepare you to select appropriate statistical models or to use them. However, you can understand the results of statistical models and the types of questions you should ask to ensure that the model being used is appropriate: Does the model selected reflect the shape of the observed data? Is there a distribution you can observe to see trends in the data?

BAYESIAN STATISTICS: WHY YOU'LL HEAR IT AND WHAT YOU SHOULD KNOW

The inferential statistics you have learned so far in this book are considered classic or frequentist. The central component of a frequentist approach is to test using hypotheses and confidence intervals and understand results as part of repeated iterations of a test to find the true population mean. Bayesian statistics, named after statistician Thomas Bayes, is an alternative school of statistical inference. It is used for conditional probabilities and tells you how to recalculate the probability that a hypothesis is true given the availability of additional data. You may hear about Bayesian statistics as the use of this approach has become increasingly popular. Bayesian statistics are often the foundational math behind some of the models currently being used in the calculation of prison sentences or suitability for jobs (see chapter 5).

PRIORS

Bayesian statistics uses priors—prior experience, knowledge, or assumptions of probabilities that have been true in the past. One critique of Bayesian statistics is that the use of assumptions introduces subjectivity into the analysis. To analyze results of this method, you must understand assumptions made to set the prior. Does the analysis use data from prior distributions with transparent data? If not, the justification for the level of the prior should be strong.

Bayesian Statistics in Practice

You are working in a community health center considering programming to reduce drug and alcohol consumption among patients. Over the past couple of months, one of your staff members has been using a different approach with clients and collecting data on the results. You can see from the mean consumption levels (drinks per week) that the intervention seems promising and you calculated an effect size of 0.2. You decide to test the intervention with a larger sample of all patients across three community health centers. Using the non-Bayesian tools you have learned in this book, you would set up a t-test with a large enough sample size or power to find a statistically significant result. You would then compare the mean results for each group to see if the p-value reaches the threshold of .05. You would ignore the promising results for the months when the staff member was using this intervention with a small subset of clients. The experiment is a clean slate from the point when it began.

A Bayesian approach would instead use the parameters from the promising work already done with this intervention to create a prior with an effect size of 0.2, possibly simulating thousands of versions of the experiment with a computer program. These data are incorporated into the analysis of the new, larger experiment. Doing this lowers the standard error because the prior is incorporated, which makes finding a statistically significant result more likely.

If instead of using the exact same intervention in the larger experiment, you had tweaked the experiment in a way you thought would make it even better, then using the data from the initial tests of the intervention would not be appropriate. A Bayesian analysis would only be appropriate if the original structure of the intervention were maintained.

Bayesian statistics can be a powerful tool with many applications. As with any tool, you must use this approach carefully. The use of priors means that two statisticians who are using the same data could come to different conclusions about the likelihood of an outcome based on the data they believe is relevant to include in the prior.

Bayesian models do not use many of the tools you have learned about in this book. There is no null hypothesis, no alternative hypothesis, no Type I and Type II errors, and no confidence interval, which can make assessing the usefulness of reported results more difficult. When reading academic studies, or even popular news articles, based on Bayesian statistics, be extra cautious about whether the researchers have any biases (conscious or unconscious) that may be affecting their prior assumptions and thus their models' outcomes.

CONCLUSION

You now have many tools for considering academic literature, understanding experiments, and using statistics in your practice. With any of the material you have learned, especially these advanced concepts, the key takeaway is not to be intimidated by complex math. No matter how complex, the math still ties back to basic concepts you have learned. Plus, remember you bring a valuable, and oftentimes unique, perspective to statistics. Be wary of assumptions and biases in math, just as you are wary of assumptions and biases in your practice.

KEY TAKEAWAYS

- Unless you are confident an effect is only going to occur in one direction and there are no risks to disregarding the possibility that the effect will be different from what you assume, then you should use a two-tailed test.
- Bayesian models can incorporate prior knowledge about an intervention and increase the likelihood of finding statistical significance, but you should be careful to examine the assumptions used in the prior.
- While $p < .05$ can be a useful threshold for identifying promising results, it may not mean the results will be replicable. An effect size can be a useful check on the p-value.

CHECK YOUR UNDERSTANDING

1. In the following examples, would a one-tailed or two-tailed test be more appropriate?
   a. You have developed a new intervention for schoolchildren with behavioral issues in the classroom. Your intervention is less time-consuming than the existing model, and you believe it is no less effective. You do not care if the model is more effective because if it is only equally effective, teachers will save time.
   b. You want to know if providing daily reports to parents on student behavior improves student behavior in the classroom. There are two classes of fifth grade

students. You will send daily reports home for one class but not for the other class.

2. True or False: A study that finds $p > .05$ is just as likely to be published as a study that finds $p < .05$.

3. True or False: Results from previous studies can affect your results when using Bayesian models.

APPENDIX I

GLOSSARY

ALPHA (α) The critical probability level used to decide whether to reject or accept the null hypothesis; see *significance*.

ALTERNATIVE HYPOTHESIS A statement that there is a relationship between variables.

ANOVA (F) A statistical test that determines whether there is a statistically significant difference among multiple groups (more than two).

BIAS A prejudice toward one outcome or another. In statistics, it could be underestimating the characteristics of a population based on those of a given sample.

CATEGORICAL VARIABLE A variable with two or more categories, but no intrinsic ordering to the categories.

CAUSE-AND-EFFECT RELATIONSHIP Also known as a causal relationship, this is a relationship in which one variable is the cause of change in another variable. Correlation is not sufficient to establish a causal relationship, but inferential statistical tests can.

CENTRAL LIMIT THEOREM A theory that states that given a large enough sample size from a population with limited variance, the mean of all samples from that population will be approximately equal to the mean of the population as a whole.

CHI-SQUARE (χ^2) A statistical test that determines whether what is observed in a distribution of frequencies would be what is expected to occur by chance.

COEFFICIENT OF DETERMINATION (r^2) The percent of the variance in the dependent variable that is predictable based on the independent variable.

CONFIDENCE INTERVAL A range of values that can be assumed to contain the population mean a certain percentage of the time—for example, 95 percent or 99 percent.

CONTINUOUS VARIABLE A variable that could theoretically have an infinite number of values between adjacent units.

CONTROL GROUP The group in an experiment that does not receive the treatment or experimental variable.

CONVENIENCE SAMPLE A type of nonprobability sampling in which a sample is taken from participants who are easily accessible but may not be representative of the population.

CORRELATION A measurement of the direction and degree of a relationship or association between variables.

CORRELATION TABLE A table showing correlation coefficients of variables.

DEGREES OF FREEDOM (DF) An approximation of the sample size.

DEPENDENT VARIABLE A variable that has a consequent role in relation to the independent variable.

DESCRIPTIVE STATISTICS Describes the distribution and relationship among variables. Used to organize and describe characteristics of a collection of data.

DICHOTOMOUS VARIABLE A variable that has only two categories.

DIRECT RELATIONSHIP When the relationship between two variables causes them to move in the same direction—for example, while one increases the other also increases.

DIRECTIONAL HYPOTHESIS A prediction about the type of difference between experimental and control groups indicating whether the difference will be positive or negative.

DISCRETE VARIABLE Where there are no possible values between adjacent units on the scale or only integers are included.

EFFECT SIZE (D) A measure of how different two groups are from one another. It is a measure of the magnitude of the treatment.

EMPIRICAL RESEARCH Studies that are based on things or experiences that can be observed or measured, in which knowledge is derived from experience over theory.

EXPERIMENTAL GROUP The group that is exposed to the independent or treatment variable.

FREQUENCY The number of times an event occurred in an experiment or study.

HYPOTHESIS A proposed explanation for a phenomenon based on prior knowledge.

INDEPENDENT VARIABLE A variable that has an antecedent or causal role.

INFERENTIAL STATISTICS A test used to make inferences from a smaller set of data to a larger one and estimate conclusions that extend beyond the immediate data.

INTERQUARTILE RANGE (IQR) A measure of variability based on dividing a dataset into quartiles.

INTERVAL A level of data in which the values in a dataset not only have the directionality of the ordinal level of measurement but the distance or amount between each point on the scale is the same. The zero point for this type of variable is arbitrarily set at some starting point rather than being a true zero.

INVERSE RELATIONSHIP When the relationship between two variables causes them to move in opposite directions—for example, while one increases the other decreases.

LIKERT SCALE A scale used to measure attitudes or other information on a spectrum. It is a common ordinal-level type of scale but is often treated as numerical or ratio.

MARGIN OF ERROR A measure to indicate how much your results differ from the real population value.

MEAN (M) A measure of central tendency calculated by adding all the data points in a dataset together and then dividing by the number of data points in the dataset.

MEDIAN A measure of central tendency defined by the middle value in a dataset.

MODE A measure of central tendency defined by the most frequently occurring value in a dataset.

NEGATIVE SKEW When a distribution has a long tail to the left or when the mean is less than the median for the distribution.

NOMINAL A level of data that uses nonnumerical labels for data. Where numerical values are used, they do not reflect any sort of order; they are just stand-ins for names.

NONDIRECTIONAL HYPOTHESIS A prediction about the type of difference between an experimental and control group where it is not clear if the difference will be positive or negative, only that there will be a difference.

NORMAL CURVE A distribution that is bell-shaped and symmetrical. See also *normal distribution*.

NORMAL DISTRIBUTION A function that represents the spread of many random variables as a symmetrical bell-shaped graph in which few points fall at the extremes and most are gathered around a midpoint. See also *normal curve*.

NULL HYPOTHESIS A statement of equality that says the groups being considered are the same. It is the logical counterpart of the alternative hypothesis.

ORDINAL A level of data in which the values in a dataset, whether numerical or nonnumerical, can be rank-ordered.

OUTLIER An observation point that is distant from other observations.

P-VALUE (*p*) The probability used in hypothesis testing to reject or accept the null hypothesis. See *significance*.

PARAMETER A number that quantifies a characteristic of the population.

PEARSON'S *r* A numerical index that reflects the relationship between two variables. The correlation coefficient ranges from −1 to +1.

PERCENTAGE (%) A rate, number, or amount out of 100.

POPULATION (*N*) The complete set of individuals, objects, or scores that researchers may be interested in studying.

POSITIVE SKEW When a distribution has a long tail to the right or when the mean is greater than the median for the distribution.

POST HOC TEST Testing done after finding a statistically significant result to identify the causal variable.

PRE/POST TEST A test for the differences between two means using the t-statistic that represents observations made of a single group at two points in time.

PROPORTION A part of a whole. Generally described as a portion of 1.

QUALITATIVE RESEARCH Studies that are concerned with understanding the qualities of entities, processes, and meanings that are not experimentally examined or measured in terms of quantity, amount, intensity, or frequency.

QUANTITATIVE RESEARCH Studies that are concerned with measurement and numbers. They emphasize the measurement and analysis of causal relationships between variables, not processes.

RANDOM CLUSTER SAMPLING A type of sampling in which the population is divided into clusters and then a random selection of clusters is used as the sample.

RANGE The difference between the highest and lowest scores in a distribution.

RATIO A level of data that has the directionality of ordinal-level measurements, equal distances between points, and a zero point that means a complete absence. It is the most useful level of measurement for conducting statistical tests.

SAMPLE (n) A subset of units that are drawn from a larger population.

SAMPLING ERROR The difference between the characteristics of a sample and the larger population the sample is drawn from.

SCATTERGRAM Similar to a line graph in that it uses horizontal and vertical axes but plots data points rather than a line.

SIGNIFICANCE The risk associated with being certain that what occurred was because of the treatment or intervention. The most common level of statistical significance is .05. This is the degree of risk in rejecting the null hypothesis when it is true. See also *alpha*.

SIMPLE RANDOM SAMPLE A type of sampling in which the selection of each member of a sample is entirely based on chance.

SKEW A measure of the asymmetry of a distribution around the mean in which the number of units with a value above the mean is not equal to the number of units with a value below the mean. A distribution may be positively skewed or negatively skewed.

SPURIOUS CORRELATION A relationship between two variables that appear to be related to each other but are not.

STANDARD DEVIATION (σ) The most commonly used measure to quantify the amount of spread, variation, or dispersion in a dataset.

STANDARD ERROR OF THE MEAN The standard deviation of the sampling distribution of the mean.

STATISTIC A number that quantifies a characteristic of the sample.

STATISTICAL POWER A measurement of how likely it is that you will detect an effect when it occurs.

STRATIFIED RANDOM SAMPLING A type of random sampling in which the samples in each stratum have some specific characteristic and are proportionate to the occurrence of that characteristic in the population.

T - TEST A statistical test that determines whether there is a statistically significant difference between two groups.

TYPE I ERROR (α) A decision to reject the null hypothesis when the null hypothesis is true.

TYPE II ERROR (β) A decision to retain the null hypothesis when the null hypothesis is false.

VARIABLE A property or characteristic of some event, object, or person that may have different values at different times depending on the condition.

VARIANCE The standard deviation squared.

VOLUNTEERISM A problem with sampling from volunteers that makes a sample biased because the characteristics of people who volunteer to participate differ from those of people who do not volunteer.

APPENDIX II

ANSWER KEY FOR REVIEW QUESTIONS

CHAPTER 2

1. A proportion describes a value in relation to a whole, a sample, or a population. A percentage does the same but expresses the value as a fraction of 100.

2. $$198 \div 450$$
$$= 0.44 \times 100$$
$$= 44\%$$

3. a. Nominal. Gender is a nominal-level measurement because nominal variables distinguish between two or more classes of a variable using names. There is no order associated with nominal variables.

   b. Ratio. Age is a ratio-level measurement because the difference between the values is meaningful and there is an absolute zero value.

   c. Ordinal. Level of difficulty is an ordinal-level measurement. It uses levels in order of magnitude, but the distance between levels is not clearly measureable or equivalent to certain values. Something that is impossible may not be twice as difficult as something that is only difficult.

d. Ratio. The rate of depression is a ratio-level measurement because the difference between values is meaningful and there is an absolute zero value where no instance of depression exists.

e. Interval. Test scores on a standardized test like the SAT are interval-level measurements. They use standardized scores where there is equal distance between consecutive scale points, so you can determine how many units higher or lower one case is than another. There is no absolute zero for tests like the SAT. The zero used for the test does not represent a true absence of aptitude or intelligence.

4. Ratio-level data

CHAPTER 3

1. Mean = 32.86
   Median = 32
   Mode = 32

2. Yes, it is slightly skewed because the mean is greater than the median.

3. a. Positively skewed
   b. Positively skewed
   c. Positively skewed

CHAPTER 4

1. 93

2.
$$IQR = Q_3 - Q_1$$
$$= 23 - 9$$
$$= 14$$

3. b

4. 68%

5. $SD = \sqrt{\dfrac{\Sigma(x_i - M)^2}{n}}$

$M = \dfrac{16 + 12 + 19 + 23 + 25 + 18 + 1 + 24 + 7 + 5}{10} = \dfrac{150}{10} = 15$

$$SD = \sqrt{\dfrac{\Sigma(x_i - M)^2}{n}}$$

$$= \sqrt{\dfrac{\begin{aligned}(16-15)^2 + (12-15)^2 + (19-15)^2 + (23-15)^2 + (25-15)^2 + \\ (18-15)^2 + (1-15)^2 + (24-15)^2 + (7-15)^2 + (5-15)^2\end{aligned}}{10}}$$

$$= \sqrt{\dfrac{\begin{aligned}(1)^2 + (-3)^2 + (4)^2 + (8)^2 + (10)^2 + (3)^2 + (-14)^2 + (9)^2 + \\ (-8)^2 + (-10)^2\end{aligned}}{10}}$$

$$= \sqrt{\dfrac{1 + 9 + 16 + 64 + 100 + 9 + 196 + 81 + 64 + 100}{10}}$$

$$= \sqrt{\dfrac{640}{10}} = \sqrt{64} = 8$$

(If you calculate SD using Excel, the formula uses $n-1$ instead of n. You would get a result of 8.43 rather than 8. This is a more conservative estimate of standard deviation.)

CHAPTER 5

1. a. 0.45
   b. 0.67
   c. −0.72

2. a. 5%
    b. 45%
    c. 0%
    d. 79%
3. 0.70
4. 28%

$$r = 0.53$$
$$r^2 = 0.53 \times 0.53 = 0.2809 \times 100 = 28\%$$

5. Unemployment rate
6. Population size and unemployment rate

CHAPTER 6

1. Random sampling
2. a. Convenience
    b. Random cluster sample
    c. Stratified random sample
3. 16–25: 147
    26–40: 105
    41–65: 98
4. False
5. $Standard\ Error\ of\ the\ Mean = \dfrac{s}{\sqrt{n}}$

$$= \dfrac{5}{\sqrt{150}}$$

$$= \dfrac{5}{12.25}$$

$$= 0.41$$

The confidence interval of 95 percent is 30 − (0.41 × 2) to 30 + (0.41 × 2)

$= 30 - 0.82$ to $30 + 0.82$

$= 29.18$ to 30.82

CHAPTER 7

1. a. H_0: The literacy program has no effect on scores on the standardized reading test.

   H_1: The literacy program increases scores on the standardized reading test.

   or

   H_1: The literacy program affects scores on the standardized reading test.

   b. Independent t-test

   c. $p < 0.05$

2. a. Independent

   b. Dependent

   c. Dependent

3. a. Type II

   b. Type I

4. b

5.
$$\text{Cohen's } d = \frac{20 - 15}{(2 + 4) / 2}$$

$$\text{Cohen's } d = \frac{5}{3}$$

$$\text{Cohen's } d = 1.67$$

6. Are the following effect sizes considered small, medium, or large?

   a. Large

   b. Large

c. Small

d. Medium

7. False. A large effect size does not guarantee that the practical implications will be meaningful.

CHAPTER 8

1. a. Dependent t-test

    b. ANOVA

    c. Dependent t-test

    d. Chi-sqaure

2. Two-way ANOVA

3. Yes, $p < .05$ would be a statistically significant result.

4. A t-test is the same as doing an ANOVA on two groups; $F = t^2$.

CHAPTER 9

1. a. One-tailed

    b. Two-tailed

2. False

3. True

APPENDIX III

EQUATIONS CHEAT SHEET

Coefficient of determination	r^2
Cohen's d	$= \dfrac{x_1 - x_2}{(SD_1 + SD_2)/2}$
	$= \dfrac{\text{Mean of the experimental group} - \text{Mean of the control group}}{\text{Pooled standard deviation}}$
Mean[1]	$= \dfrac{\sum x_i}{N}$
Outlier	$= 1.5(IQR)$
	$= 1.5(Q3 - Q1)$
	An observation is an outlier if it falls more that $1.5(IQR)$ above the upper quartile or $1.5(IQR)$ below the lower quartile.
Skew	$= (\text{Mean} - \text{Median})/\text{Standard deviation}$
Standard deviation	$= \dfrac{\sqrt{\sum(x_i - M)^2}}{n}$

1. Greek letters (μ and σ) are used when referring to population values like the mean and standard deviation; roman letters ($\bar{x}$ and S or SD) are used when referring to a sample.

Σ (sigma) indicates that you should take the sum of the terms that follow

x_i = each individual score

M = the mean of all scores

n = the sample size (can also be seen as N, which refers to the population size)

Standard error of the mean $= \dfrac{s}{\sqrt{n}}$

Variance $= \dfrac{\Sigma(x_i - M)^2}{n}$

Σ (sigma) indicates that you should take the sum of the terms that follow

x_i = each individual score

M = the mean of all scores

n = the sample size (can also be seen as N, which refers to the population size)

REFERENCES

Arnett, Jeffrey J. 2008. "The Neglected 95 Percent: Why American Psychology Needs to Become Less American." *American Psychologist* 63(7): 602–614. https://doi.org/10.1037/0003-066X.63.7.602.

Donohue, John J., III, and Steven D. Levitt. 2001. "The Impact of Legalized Abortion on Crime." *Quarterly Journal of Economics* 116(2): 379–420. https://doi.org/10.1162/00335530151144050.

Fraser, Mark W., Maeda J. Galinsky, and Jack M. Richman. 1999. "Risk, Protection, and Resilience: Toward a Conceptual Framework for Social Work Practice." *Social Work Research* 23(3): 131–143. https://doi.org/10.1093/swr/23.3.131.

Greeno, Catherine G., Tina Zimmerman, Morgen Kelly, Addie Weaver, and Carol M. Anderson. 2012. "'What Is Therapy?' A Therapist-Developed Intervention to Reduce Missed Appointments in Community Mental Health." *Social Work in Mental Health* 10(1): 1–11. https://doi.org/10.1080/15332985.2011.620506.

Hatfield, Elaine, and Susan Sprecher. 1986. "Measuring Passionate Love in Intimate Relations." *Journal of Adolescence* 9(4): 383–410. https://doi.org/10.1016/S0140-1971(86)80043-4.

Hendrick, Clyde, and Susan Hendrick. 1986. "A Theory and Method of Love." *Journal of Personality and Social Psychology* 50(2): 392–402. https://doi.org/10.1037/0022-3514.50.2.392.

REFERENCES

Henrich, Joseph, Steven J. Heine, and Ara Norenzayan. 2010. "The Weirdest People in the World?" *Behavioral and Brain Sciences* 33(2–3): 61–83; discussion 83–135. https://doi.org/10.1017/S0140525X0999152X.

Hsieh, Ching-Chi, and M. D. Pugh. 1993. "Poverty, Income Inequality, and Violent Crime: A Meta-Analysis of Recent Aggregate Data Studies." *Criminal Justice Review* 18(2): 182–202. https://doi.org/10.1177/073401689301800203.

Kelling, George L., and William H. Sousa. 2001. "Do Police Matter? An Analysis of the Impact of New York City's Police Reforms." Civic Report No. 22. Manhattan Institute.

Magnuson, Katherine, and Elizabeth Votruba-Drzal. 2009. "Enduring Influences of Childhood." *Focus* 26(2): 32–37. https://www.irp.wisc.edu/publications/focus/pdfs/foc262f.pdf.

Manning, Jennifer. 2018. "Membership of the 115th Congress: A Profile." Congressional Research Service. https://www.senate.gov/CRSpubs/b8f6293e-c235-40fd-b895-6474d0f8e809.pdf.

Nevin, Rick. 2000. "How Lead Exposure Relates to Temporal Changes in IQ, Violent Crime, and Unwed Pregnancy." *Environmental Research* 83(1): 1–22. https://doi.org/10.1006/enrs.1999.4045.

Shlonsky, Aron, and Leonard Gibbs. 2004. "Will the Real Evidence-Based Practice Please Stand Up? Teaching the Process of Evidence-Based Practice to the Helping Professions." *Brief Treatment and Crisis Intervention* 4(2): 137–153. https://pdfs.semanticscholar.org/f9d4/7545014166b07df209af028c3f62fe1cc91a.pdf.

Silver, Nate. 2012. *The Signal and the Noise: Why Most Predictions Fail—but Some Don't*. New York: Penguin.

Skogan, Wesley, and Kathleen Frydl, eds. 2004. *Fairness and Effectiveness in Policing: The Evidence*. Washington, DC: National Academies Press.

Sternberg, Robert J. 1986. "A Triangular Theory of Love." *Psychological Review* 93: 119–135. https://doi.org/10.1037//0033-295X.93.2.119.

Vigen, Tyler. 2015. *Spurious Correlations*. New York: Hachette. http://www.tylervigen.com/.

REFERENCES

Weitzman, Beth C., Tod Mijanovich, Carolyn Berry, Maggie Giorgio, and Maggie Paul. 2017. "Evaluation of the Corporation for Supportive Housing's Social Innovation Fund Initiative: Final Report." Corporation for Supportive Housing, August 2017. https://www.nationalservice.gov/sites/default/files/evidenceexchange/CSH_Final_Report_v1_081417_508.pdf.

CPSIA information can be obtained
at www.ICGtesting.com
Printed in the USA
LVHW110708141020
668718LV00002B/2